What the experts are saying about
One Minute Mysteries: 65 Short Mysteries You Solve With Science!

"Conundrums, puzzles and enigmas! The scientific approach prevails overall. *One Minute Mysteries: 65 Short Mysteries You Solve With Science!* turns us into sleuth hounds. If only textbooks were such fun!"
> —April Holladay, author of *Globe and Mail*'s online science column, *Wonder Quest*

"*One Minute Mysteries: 65 Short Mysteries You Solve With Science!* turns kids into scientists! Each of these clever stories sets up a mystery that can be solved using a bit of creative analytical reasoning. Stimulating and great fun for the whole family!"
> —Katrina L. Kelner, Ph.D., Deputy Editor of Life Sciences, *Science* Magazine

"Parents and kids alike will be challenged by these stimulating, real-world science mysteries. *One Minute Mysteries: 65 Short Mysteries You Solve With Science!* is a great way to grow a young scientist—or improve an old one! This book belongs in every school and every home."
> —Julie Edmonds, Co-Director, Carnegie Academy for Science Education

"Everyone loves a mystery! The father-daughter team behind *One Minute Mysteries: 65 Short Mysteries You Solve With Science!* has done a wonderful job writing stories that draw in curious young people... and show them that science can answer many of life's mysteries!"
> —Patricia Sievert, MS, Physics and Physics Education, Northern Illinois University

"A wonderful novel way to get kids happily engaged in problem-solving. It not only teaches kids about science, but also demonstrates how to use science in everyday life. Relevant, real-life examples make *One Minute Mysteries: 65 Short Mysteries You Solve With Science!* a great read for kids...and adults!"
> —Marina Moses, DrPH, George Washington University School of Public Health and Health Services

"These clever little science-based mysteries will have a myriad of uses. I see them as the perfect solution for stimulating kids on car journeys by really getting them to use their intellect."
> —Kathleen Karr, author of *Born for Adventure* and *Agath* nning *The 7th Knot*

"Like potato chips, one isn't enough—with *One Minute Mysteries: 65 Short Mysteries You Solve With Science!* you'll just want to read more: These one-minute science mysteries are fun treats for readers that will sharpen their powers of observation and improve their reasoning abilities."
—Brenda Seabrooke, author of award-winning *The Haunting of Swain's Fancy*

"An extraordinary, one-of-a-kind catalyst for science enthusiasm – and in just 60 seconds each!"
—Margaret Kenda, Ph.D., author of *Science Wizardry for Kids* and *Math Wizardry for Kids*

"Amazing, mind-bending tales so interesting you don't even realize you are learning! I couldn't stop reading the book."
—Billy Moses, fifth grader, Washington, DC

"Brilliant idea! What a wonderful father-daughter venture! The short story form and lively, friendly writing style make reading easy and fun. I couldn't put it down! When I thought I'd take a break from reading, my curiosity led me to read 'just one more.' *One Minute Mysteries: 65 Short Mysteries You Solve With Science!* is not too theoretical, is easy to apply and boosts children's natural curiosity to learn."
—Shoshana Hayman, Life Center, Tel Aviv

"*One Minute Mysteries: 65 Short Mysteries You Solve With Science!* is a great concept! It puts science in an everyday context and mixes it with a little intrigue to draw in both the inquisitive mystery buff and the curious budding scientist. What a brilliant idea for a father and daughter to write them together. They ensure that the mysteries are just as engaging for adults as they are for kids. What a great book!"
—Mark Zev, author of *101 Things Everyone Should Know About Math*

"I love *One Minute Mysteries: 65 Short Mysteries You Solve With Science!* I'm delighted to see a book featuring critical reasoning rather than fact memorization offered as a science-education resource. This book keeps you turning page after page!"
—Ryan McAllister, Ph.D., Biophysics, Georgetown University

"*One Minute Mysteries: 65 Short Mysteries You Solve With Science!* gives parents and children a magnificent imaginative platform to discover the way our world works."
—Marisa Frieder, Ph.D., Microbiology, Oregon Health and Science University

Science, Naturally!®

Teaching the science of everyday life

One Minute Mysteries:
65 Short Mysteries You Solve With Science!

Eric Yoder and Natalie Yoder

Science, Naturally!®
Washington, DC

Copyright © 2008 Science, Naturally! and Eric Yoder and Natalie Yoder
First edition • September 2008 • ISBN: 978-0-9678020-1-5
Second edition • June 2009
E-book edition • March 2009 • ISBN: 978-0-9700106-7-4

Published in the United States by:
Science, Naturally!® LLC
725 Eighth Street, SE
Washington, DC 20003
202-465-4798 / Toll-free: 1-866-SCI-9876 (1-866-724-9876)
Fax: 202-558-2132
Info@ScienceNaturally.com / www.ScienceNaturally.com

Distributed to the book trade in the United States by:
National Book Network
(301) 459-3366 / Toll-free: 800-787-6859 / Fax: 301.429.5746
CustServ@nbnbooks.com / www.nbnbooks.com

Senior Editor: Stine Bauer Dahlberg, Washington, DC
Associate Editors: Emily Schuster, Silver Spring, MD
                     Jessica Wilde, Washington, DC
                     Tracey Kilby, Washington, DC
                     Elaine Simeon, Potomac, MD

Cover, Book Design and Section Illustrations by Andrew Barthelmes, Peekskill, NY

Library of Congress Cataloging-in-Publication Data

Yoder, Eric.
  One Minute Mysteries: 65 Short Mysteries You Solve With Science! / by Eric Yoder and Natalie
Yoder. — 1st ed.
    p. cm.
  Includes index.
  ISBN-13: 978-0-9678020-1-5
  ISBN-10: 0-9678020-1-6
  1. Science—Miscellanea. 2. Science—Study and teaching (Middle school) 3. Detective and
mystery stories, American I. Yoder, Natalie, 1993- II. Title.
  Q173.Y63 2007
  500—dc22
                              2006037879
11 10 9 8 7 6 5 4 3 2

FSC
Mixed Sources
Product group from well-managed
forests and other controlled sources

Cert no. SW-COC-002283
www.fsc.org
© 1996 Forest Stewardship Council

Schools, libraries, government and non-profit organizations can receive a bulk discount for quantity orders.
Please contact us at the address above or email us at Info@ScienceNaturally.com.

Printed in the United States of America

Table of Contents

BONUS SECTION
Five More Minutes of Mysteries! ●————(143)

Discover *One Minute Mysteries: 65 Short Mysteries You Solve With Math!* ●————(155)

Why I Wrote This Book—
by Eric Yoder

This book began with stories I wrote just for the fun of it. I was hoping to spur my daughter Natalie's interest in science and help her see that science is far more than academic. I wanted to emphasize its widespread, real-life applications—that is, that we can all be scientists in daily life. Mysteries seemed to be the perfect vehicle.

Soon she started writing stories on her own to try to stump me. After we had accumulated a number of them between us, it became clear that the stories could be the basis of a book. From that point, we wrote side by side, typically with one of us getting the original idea—usually from something we observed in everyday life—and developing it together. Those sessions were springboards for many discussions, and not just about science. If you want to get to know someone, write a book with her!

Natalie also kept the behavior and dialogue of the characters authentic; how far off track my suggestions were directly correlated to how much her eyes rolled.

We hope that you enjoy reading these mysteries as much as we enjoyed writing them!

–Eric

September 2008

Why I Wrote This Book–
by Natalie Yoder

Hello. My name is Natalie Yoder. When I'm not doing sports, cleaning my room, spending time with my friends or working on homework, I write with my dad.

I started writing stories when I was about eight. My favorite genre was mysteries, so, of course, my first stories were mysteries. I called them *The Clubhouse Gang*, and they starred my five best friends. Ever since, I have been writing mystery stories for fun with my dad.

One day, Dad came to me and asked if I'd like to work with him on a book—and get it published! I thought that would be really cool! At first I was a little worried about how much work it would be, but once I got into it, it was really fun.

First, we had to think of ideas for our mysteries. Then we had to write so many of them. Lots of times we were just stuck, wondering how we were going to come up with yet another idea. We ended up with this really weird technique. We stared at a dead spider on the ceiling above my dad's desk for hours and hours. I don't know why, but just staring at the spider gave us ideas.

Even though the writing process was hard, in the end it was all worth it. Writing stories helped me express myself, and it even helped me get closer to my dad. I think everyone has stories inside of them. Whatever they are, you should think about writing them down.

—Natalie

September 2008

Life Science

Classified Information

"Lions and tigers and bears, oh my!" the students laughed as they climbed onto the school bus on a warm, sunny day for a field trip to the zoo.

The happy mood quickly left when Carlos pulled out an article he'd clipped from that morning's newspaper. Several animals had been stolen from the zoo the night before, and the police suspected that someone was pretending to be a zoo employee to get keys to the cages.

Valerie, Meredith and Carlos decided to investigate while they visited the animals they were assigned to write about.

"Excuse me," Valerie said to the woman working at the main information desk. "Where would I go to see the bats?"

"The bird house, right up this path," the woman said.

Meanwhile, Meredith was disappointed when she arrived at the polar bear exhibit. No bears were to be seen, since they were all back in their cave.

"Can't you get the bears to come out?" she asked the zookeeper.

"I'm afraid they won't come out on a day like this," he said.

Carlos was also disappointed when he reached the owls, which were just sitting on their perches.

"I was hoping to see them fly," he said to a zookeeper there.

"I'm sorry, but you'd have to come back tonight to see that," the woman replied.

When they gathered at the bus to return to school, they shared their experiences. Valerie whispered to their teacher, Ms. Peralta, "I know who's been pretending to be a zoo employee."

"Who?" Ms. Peralta asked.

Ms. Peralta took Valerie to see a security guard. "Tell him what you told me," Ms. Peralta said.

Valerie said, "Meredith asked the zookeeper at the polar bear cage to bring out the bears, but it's too hot for them and it would be very dangerous to try to get a bear out of its cave. And Carlos was disappointed that the owls weren't moving, but owls are nocturnal. That means that they sleep during the day and become active at night. Those zookeepers knew what they were talking about. But you ought to investigate the woman at the information desk. She told me to go to the bird house to find bats. Bats aren't birds, they're mammals, and anyone who is really a zoo employee would know that."

Food for Thought

It was the "End of the Pleistocene Epoch Party" and half the students had been assigned to decorate the room, while the others brought in food, all with an Ice Age theme.

After they finished doing cave drawings on the blackboard, Kyrie, Taylor and Emma walked around to check out the food.

Kyrie looked at a punch bowl full of some red liquid. It smelled like regular punch, but she wasn't so sure. It was thicker than punch and warm.

"What's that stuff?" she asked Zackery.

"Woolly mammoth blood!" he said.

"Ewwwww!" Kyrie said.

"Try this 'giant deer' meat. It's real venison my dad got from a hunter," Derek said.

"Ugh!" she said.

At the next table, Emma saw something that kind of smelled like salmon, but was as tough as leather. "What's this?" she asked Cameron.

"Dried, smoked fish, of course," Cameron said. "Remember we learned that smoking meat over a fire preserves it? We could leave this out for weeks and it would taste just the same."

"Just as bad, you mean," Emma grumbled.

Taylor, meanwhile, had stopped at Daniel's table, where he was arranging a plate of cookies shaped like Stegosauruses.

"Finally, something I recognize as food," Emma said when she and Kyrie joined Taylor. "Don't you just hate it, being hungry and most of the food is so gross?"

"There's only one thing I'm not going to have, and that's because it's not realistic," Taylor said.

"Which one is that?" Kyrie asked.

"Much as I like cookies, Stegosaurus cookies don't fit in with the theme of the party," Taylor said. "Dinosaurs lived in the Triassic, Jurassic, and Cretaceous periods between 250 and 65 million years ago, meaning that they were extinct long before the Pleistocene Epoch and the Ice Age. The Pleistocene Epoch was only about 1.8 million to 10,000 years ago."

Bear Scare

At a one-week ski camp in mid-winter, three best friends were in the same group—Carla, Sasha and Elizabeth. Today their group was going on a treasure hunt for a bag of candy.

They had a map with names of the different ski trails and clues that led them to the right ones. After going down several trails and up some ski lifts, they found a tree painted with an X. Also on the tree was a large scratch mark.

"X marks the spot," Carla said.

They took off their skis and dug in the snow at the base of the tree. But there was only an empty box.

They skied down to the ski school, where they found Leslie Coyle, their instructor.

"We found the box, but there was no candy in it," Sasha said.

"I asked the workers to take out the prize because of the bears," Ms. Coyle said. "Bears can smell food even through a box and we don't want them going to the areas where there are skiers."

Elizabeth noticed a big bag of candy on Ms. Coyle's desk.

"Stealer!" Elizabeth said, laughing. "You just wanted the candy for yourself. And I can prove it."

"So, prove it," Ms. Coyle laughed. "Are you saying there are no bears in this area? Or that bears couldn't smell candy through a box?"

"There are bears here—that's what made the scratch mark on the tree," replied Elizabeth. "And bears probably could smell the candy through a box. But it's the middle of winter. Bears are hibernating now, so they wouldn't be out roaming around," Elizabeth said as they all shared the candy.

The Horse's Fodder

Horseback riding was a big part of the program at the summer camp. The campers were going to learn how to ride, tack up and groom the horses. Everyone was assigned a horse that they were expected to take special care of for the two weeks.

It was the first evening of camp, and around the dinner table, Kelsey, Drew and Malaya were very excited about their horses—Rocky, Alex and Blaze. The next day, they were going to ride the horses down to the stream that ran past the camp to wade in the water.

"Is it okay if we take a treat to our horses?" Malaya asked their counselor after dinner.

"Sure, they'd love that," said their counselor. "Except it has to be food you took for yourself but just can't finish."

After clearing the table, they wrapped some leftovers in napkins and started off toward the stables.

"If I'd known the rule, I would have saved more food for Rocky," Kelsey said. "I only had a couple of carrot sticks left."

"All I have for Alex is one apple chunk," Drew said glumly.

"Well, I saved a whole pork chop for Blaze," Malaya said.

Kelsey smiled as she said, "I know which horse is going to eat the least."

"Which one?" Drew asked.

"Horses are herbivores, not carnivores. That means they don't eat meat, just plants," Kelsey said as they reached the stables. "They'll eat carrot sticks and apples, but they won't eat pork chops. Here, Malaya, you can give some of my carrot sticks to Blaze."

"You're kidding," Dejon said.

"Nope," Damien said. "My parents told me this morning. The power's been out in the school almost the entire break."

Dejon, Matt, Quincy and Damien were walking to school on the first day back after the winter break of more than a week.

"What happened?" Matt asked.

"Dad said they were doing some kind of work on the electrical system and they had to shut down the power the whole time," Damien said. "He said it's a good thing the weather has been so mild, so at least the pipes didn't freeze and break."

As they approached the school, they could see that the lights were on. Everything seemed okay. But then Quincy realized something. "Our experiments!" he said.

For several weeks before the break, they had been doing projects that measured the effects of light on growth, using terrariums with lights on automatic timers.

Dejon had been growing bean sprouts, Matt had been growing mushrooms, Quincy had been growing cucumbers and Damien had been growing corn. It was going to be a big part of their grade for that marking period.

"What about the experiments?" Dejon asked.

"We'll have to start all over again," Quincy said. "Without those automatic lights, they'll be ruined."

"Not all of them," Damien said. "I can think of one of them that should be all right with very little light."

"Whose?" Quincy asked.

"You're in luck, Matt," Damien said. "Mushrooms don't need much light to grow. That's why you mostly find them in shady places."

Bugged by an Assignment

"You want us to make a bug collection?" Brooke asked.

"An insect collection," said Ms. Graffwalner. "It's an excellent way to learn about the diversity in nature."

Ms. Graffwalner was handing out the assignments for the fall grading period. "And get started soon. As the cold weather gets here, the insects will start dying off."

"What kind of insects should we get?" Adlai asked.

"Doesn't matter. Just so long as you capture and classify at least ten different kinds, as it says on the sheet, and do the other work you see there," said Ms. Graffwalner.

"How are we supposed to catch them?" Maureen asked.

"Any way you want. Just don't squish them. It's hard to classify a squished specimen," Ms. Graffwalner replied.

Weeks passed. From time to time, the students would talk about the project over lunch.

"There are never bugs around when you need them," Brooke said. "One day, I went to a marsh with my father. I got eaten alive by mosquitoes, but could I catch one? No. So far my only bugs are some ants I got out of a trap in our laundry room."

"I only have a couple of beetles from our garage and a dead fly I found on a windowsill," Maureen said. "My parents even bought me a butterfly net and took me to a park. I looked like an idiot chasing bugs around. How can we classify bugs when we can't even catch them?"

"I caught all mine in a couple of days in my backyard, actually," Adlai said.

"How?" Maureen asked.

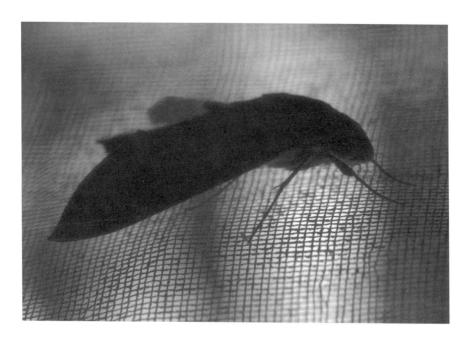

"Why chase insects when you can make them come to you?" Adlai said. "All I had to do was leave the porch light on at night. Many insects are attracted to light—there are different theories about why. In a couple of nights, I had way more different kinds than I needed—moths, beetles, mosquitoes and lots more."

It's in the Blood

7

For her birthday party, Lily and some friends went to a nature center to learn about animals of the forest. In a large tank were several frogs, motionless as they sat on the sand, and breathing slowly. Next to that tank were several tanks with snakes, crawling over rocks and over each other.

Another exhibit showed a stuffed rattlesnake curled up on a rock, with a heat lamp shining on it to simulate a sunny day. Other exhibits had live mice and rabbits.

"Now, let's play a game to see who can identify animals only by touch! Who wants to be first?" the naturalist, Mr. Bruyette, asked. "How about the birthday girl?"

Lily's friends clapped, most of them relieved that they wouldn't have to be first.

Mr. Bruyette said, "I'm going to blindfold you, and then I'll bring you an animal. You touch it and tell me what it is. Don't worry, it won't bite. And if it bites, don't worry, it won't bite hard. And if it bites hard, don't worry, it's not poisonous. Probably not, anyway," he said.

Very funny, Lily thought as he put a blindfold over her eyes.

He left her for a few moments, then came back and touched her fingertip to something. She jerked her hand away, but not before she noticed that it felt smooth, dry and warm.

"I know what it is," Lily said. "You're trying to trick me."

"Then what is it?" Mr. Bruyette asked.

With her blindfold still on, Lily explained, "It wasn't a mouse or rabbit because there was no fur. Reptiles, like snakes, and amphibians, like frogs, don't have fur, but they're cold-blooded and wouldn't feel warm to touch unless they were being heated. You got the stuffed snake from under that heat lamp and had me touch that."

Seed of an Idea

8

"Trevor, get out of the garden!" Jorge yelled.

The family had just returned from a springtime walk in the park, where there was an area for dogs to romp around in the bushes. Trevor, their beagle, had really enjoyed that.

With so many plants already in bloom, they realized it was time to plant their garden. So on the way home, they bought seeds for the vegetables they always enjoyed growing—corn, peas and cucumbers. The problem was that as soon as they dug into the moist soil, Trevor started rolling in it.

"Dogs just do that, son," Jorge's father said. "Why don't you bathe him while your sister and I plant the garden?"

Jorge's sister, Gabriella, was still in preschool. Her idea of planting was to go around the yard pulling up bits of grass and throwing them into the garden soil. As Gabriella was doing this, Jorge took Trevor into the laundry room to wash him in the large sink.

Several weeks later, the garden was starting to grow. Shoots of corn plants were coming up, and the peas and cucumber plants were putting out tiny leaves.

However, there was a problem: The garden was full of weeds. Jorge and his father had to pick them very carefully so they would not disturb the growing vegetable plants.

"I wish I knew how all these weeds got in here," Jorge muttered to his father. He paused and thought, "Actually, I do know."

"Then how did the weeds get here?" his father asked.

"Gabriella was just putting blades of grass in the dirt, and weeds don't grow from blades of grass—they grow from seeds. When Trevor was running around in the park, the seeds from the weeds there stuck to his coat," Jorge said. "That's one way seeds spread—by sticking to animals. Then, when he came home and rolled in the garden dirt, the seeds came off and started to grow here."

Shell Game

"Welcome to the science fair," Principal Russell's voice echoed through the multi-purpose room of Jackson Middle School. "This year, we will have a special surprise for all of the students. A professor from the local college will be judging our science fair."

"But something has gone wrong," Principal Russell added over the microphone. "Part of a science project has been stolen. This is very serious. If we do not find who stole it or if they don't confess, the science fair will be canceled."

As groaning filled the room, Vanessa went up to Principal Russell and asked, "What was stolen?"

"A hermit crab was stolen from Edward's science fair project," Principal Russell said. "Go see for yourself."

In Edward's project there were six different surfaces: gravel, sand, rocks, shells, leaves, and woodchips. Hermit crabs were crawling all around.

"How many hermit crabs do you have in here?" Vanessa asked, turning over a few empty shells.

"I have seven," Edward said. "I even painted the numbers on their shells. But number five is missing. Somebody must have taken him out of his shell. See?" He held up the shell numbered five for her to see that it was empty.

"What are the other shells for?" Vanessa asked.

"Just for decoration," Edward said.

"Have you ever had hermit crabs as pets?" she asked.

"No," he said.

Vanessa took the microphone and said, "The science fair is not canceled. Everybody go on like nothing happened. I know where the missing hermit crab is."

"Where?" Edward asked.

"You might not know this because you don't keep them as pets, but hermit crabs find new shells when they outgrow the ones they already have," Vanessa told him. "So number five must have moved from the shell it was in to one of the decoration shells."

Sure enough, they looked in the decoration shells and found the missing hermit crab just like Vanessa had thought.

A Question of Identity

"Watch out!" Samir yelled.

"What?" Maggie asked.

"Don't step on it! Look!" Samir said.

"Eww, yuck!" Maggie said as she lifted her foot. On the ground lay something slimy, long and skinny.

They were outside walking alongside the playground during break time, and Samir had spotted something dark in the grass just where Maggie was about to step. It was several inches long, dark in color and about as big around as a pencil. It was also dead, and a little shriveled up, so it was hard to tell exactly what it was.

Their teacher heard them and came over. "What's wrong?" Miss Geong said.

"I almost stepped on a dead snake!" Maggie said.

Miss Geong took a stick and poked at it. "It could be a small snake, or maybe just a large worm," she said.

"Whatever it is, let's just leave it here," Maggie said.

"I can't do that," Miss Geong said. "If it's a snake, there could be a whole lot more. I'll have to tell the principal to cancel all recesses until an expert comes."

"No, we can figure this out ourselves," Samir said. "Is it okay if we take a closer look at it?"

"Yes, since it's dead," Miss Geong said. "But how do you expect to tell what it is?"

They picked up the dead, unknown thing with the stick, put it into a bag and carried it into the science room. There Samir got a sharp knife and cut it open. "The playground doesn't have to be closed," he said. "This cannot be a snake because a snake has a backbone—it's a vertebrate. Worms do not have backbones—they're invertebrates. This does not have a backbone, so it must be just a large worm."

Turning Over a New Leaf

"I can't wait until I get to the farm," Alyssa said to her best friends, Samantha and Christie. "It stinks that we're not doing it together, though."

"It's all Miss Page's fault for splitting us up," Christie said.

The class was studying trees and other plants. Alyssa, Samantha and Christie, who did everything together, had been told to research business uses of trees. One of them was to go to an apple orchard, another to a pear orchard and another to a Christmas tree farm. Afterward, each had to produce a report.

Other kids had been assigned other types of reports on plants that involved gathering samples from parks, the arboretum and even backyards.

The day the reports were due, the students were showing each other their reports on the way to class.

Ian saw them from across the hall and noticed that they were holding their reports. He was not very friendly to the three of them because he was jealous that they were good students. He didn't see a leaf on the cover of Samantha's report, as the assignment required.

"Well, the trio isn't all going to get A's on this report," he sneered. "Looks like you didn't even do your research, Samantha. I don't see any leaf on your report, and trees have leaves! Looks like you taped a toothpick or something to it."

"That doesn't prove I didn't do my research," Samantha said. "All it proves is where I went and you should be able to figure it out, Ian."

Ms. Newlon explained, "First a butterfly lays eggs, then the egg hatches into a caterpillar, then the caterpillar makes a chrysalis and then the butterfly comes out of the chrysalis. It is quite an unusual life cycle. We call it metamorphosis. The butterfly comes out of the chrysalis fully grown, so you will never see any 'baby butterflies' flying around. What you caught was a small moth," Ms. Newlon said. "They go through a similar life cycle, but they're not butterflies. However, you still have time to do the extra credit project. If you find an example in nature of a life cycle and bring it in, that will be enough to raise your grade to an A!"

A Fishy Solution

"Man, a backyard fish pond is a lot more work than an aquarium!" Dennis said to his friend Anders.

Digging the hole for the pond was hard work, and then Dennis and his father had to set up the liner, cover it with gravel and fill it with water. Now they were ready to get the fish and put them in.

Or so they thought. The man in the fish store had a warning. "Raccoons, skunks and certain birds might treat your pond as a fast-food restaurant," he said.

Dennis told that to Anders, who had come over to see how things were going. "That could be a problem," Anders said. "I've seen raccoons around, and sometimes you smell that a skunk has been here. And there are a lot of crows."

"That's why I came up with the idea to put a cover on the pond," Dennis said, showing Anders a large sheet of clear plastic. "It had to be something that we could see through, but that would discourage anything from getting at the fish. All I have to do is cut this to the shape of the pond and lay it on top of the water. That way we'll have no problems."

"I'm not so sure about that. You might want to talk to the guy in the fish store again," Anders said. "You could be causing a bigger problem than you're solving."

"What do you mean?" Dennis asked.

"Fish need oxygen to live, just like we do," Anders said. "A lot of the oxygen that's in their water gets absorbed from the air. If you lay that plastic on top of the water, you'd be cutting off their supply of oxygen and it could kill them."

A Fair Contest

"Judging a contest can be really hard," Mr. O'Shea, the science teacher, had warned them.

And he had been right.

It was the night of the school's annual science fair. The cafeteria was filled with displays. As a reward for their own good work in science class, fifth graders John and Brian had been named the student judges for the second graders' nature dioramas.

They narrowed down their choices to three.

"I like this one," John said, pointing to a polar scene. The student who made it had been creative, using Styrofoam as an iceberg and blue plastic as water and populating the scene with penguins and polar bears.

Next John studied a jungle scene with closely packed trees filled with monkeys, birds and gorillas, and with a lion prowling underneath.

"This one is good, too," he said. "It's really lifelike."

Brian picked up a desert scene with sandpaper for sand, cactuses, lizards and a snake hiding under a rock.

"I really think this one has to be the winner," Brian said.

"Actually, that looks like it took less effort than the other two," John said.

"I agree," Brian said. "But remember, this is a science fair."

"What do you mean?" John asked.

"A polar scene has to represent either the Arctic or the Antarctic," Brian said. "Penguins are only found in the Antarctic, and polar bears are only found in the Arctic. So either way, you wouldn't have them together.

"And while the lion is called the king of the jungle, that's not where they live," he added. "They mostly live on savannahs or in open woodlands. So that display has a mistake in it, too. Only the desert scene is scientifically accurate."

Hair Style

"What is this?" Suzanne demanded, storming into Marie's room.

It was early in the morning, too early for Marie.

Suzanne always was the first one up, because she liked to take a shower, blow-dry her medium-length, brown-blonde hair, brush it and straighten it.

Marie's hair was black, much shorter and required much less care. She preferred to spend her spare time with her science kits, looking in her microscope or reading science fiction.

"What is what?" Marie mumbled, half opening her eyes.

"This!" Suzanne said, waving her hairbrush in front of Marie's face.

"Looks like your hairbrush," Marie grumbled, rolling over. Their dog Max, a long-haired dachshund, growled. It was too early for Max, too.

"You've been brushing Max with it, haven't you?" Suzanne demanded.

"What makes you think that?" Marie asked.

"There are hairs on it that don't look like mine," Suzanne said. "They're not the right color. They look more like Max's."

"If you let me sleep for five more minutes, I promise I'll prove that they're not," Marie said.

"How are you going to do that?" Suzanne asked.

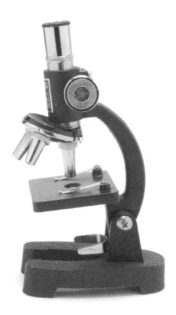

Marie got a clean comb and ran it through Suzanne's hair until a couple of hairs came out, then put them under the microscope. "If you look at your own hairs closely, you'll see they're not all exactly the same color," she told Suzanne. "But the surface texture and the pattern of the markings is the same."

Then she ran her fingers across Max's coat until some fur came off and put one of Max's hairs in the microscope.

"As you'll notice, a dog hair looks different from a human hair under a microscope—the texture is different and so are the color patterns," she said, showing Suzanne the slide. "Also, animal hairs have a lot more dark, oval shapes in them—they're called ovoid bodies, by the way.

"Now, let's check to make sure whose hair this is," Marie said. She took one of the hairs Suzanne suspected of coming from the dog and put it under the microscope. Suzanne could see that it matched her hair, not Max's.

"Always test your hypothesis before stating a conclusion," Marie said.

Earth and
Space Science

Cloudy on the Concept

"Welcome back to Henderson School for another year of learning," Principal Tucker said into the microphone to the students assembled in the gym on the first morning of the school year. "This year, instead of staying in the same room all day, you'll rotate among three new teachers who specialize in math, science and English. They have made up a special test. If you can figure out which teacher will teach which subject based on what each teacher says, you won't have to do homework for the first week."

A man who looked like he had just graduated from college took the microphone.

"I'm Mr. Banks. Since there are 71 students in your grade this year, we'll be dividing the class into three equal groups, and this will help everyone learn more good," he said.

"I'm Miss Smith," a tall woman with glasses said. "Don't worry, you'll get to know Mr. Banks and Mrs. Nicco and I very well."

A blonde woman, who had to be Mrs. Nicco, then said, "You'll all go to recess together, though, which should be no problem today since the sky is clear, except for some nimbo-cirrus clouds."

Principal Tucker took over the microphone. "Now, based on what they just said, which teacher is teaching which subject?"

Shoshana wrote on a piece of paper, handed it to the principal and put away her notebook. "I won't be doing homework until next week," she said.

"What did you write?" her friend Anna asked.

Shoshana explained to her friends after school. "They were playing a game with us by making mistakes on purpose that no teacher who knows a subject would make," she said.

"Mrs. Nicco couldn't be the new science teacher, since there's no such thing as nimbo-cirrus clouds.

"Miss Smith couldn't be the new English teacher, since the correct expression would have been 'you'll get to know Mr. Banks and Mrs. Nicco and me very well.'

"Mr. Banks couldn't be the new math teacher, since three doesn't divide evenly into 71. He also couldn't be the English teacher, since he said 'learn more good,' when the correct phrase is 'learn better.' That meant Mr. Banks was the science teacher.

"That left only the math teacher or the English teacher as options. Since we knew Miss Smith wasn't the English teacher, she had to be the math teacher. That means Mrs. Nicco is the English teacher."

17

Shadow of a Doubt

"Are you sure this is where it fell off?" Sanya asked.

"Of course I'm sure," Megan said. Several of her friends had gathered around her in a corner of the athletic field on a sunny day. "When the bell rang to end recess, I was standing right here."

"The ten o'clock recess, you mean?" Delaney asked.

"Right," Megan said.

It was now the two o'clock recess. They had only a few minutes before the bell would sound again to call them back into school. After school the field would be full of players coming for soccer practice. Once the field got trampled by so many feet, there would be little chance of finding Megan's lost earring.

"Tell us exactly what happened," Karin said.

"I was standing right here, brushing my hair, and I saw a glint of light flying in front of me. It must have been the earring coming off. I saw it fall into my shadow, right where the shadow of my head was. But I didn't have time to look for it."

Several more girls started searching the spot where the head of Megan's shadow was falling. "Aren't you going to help look?" one of them called to Karin, who was glancing at a sunny patch of ground off to the side.

"Why should I look over there when I've already found it over here?" she asked.

"But it fell where my shadow is, and my shadow is right here. How did the earring get over there?" asked Megan.

"The earring didn't move, but the shadow did," Karin said. "Think of a sundial. The shadow will move as the day goes on. Where Megan's shadow is falling now, at two in the afternoon, is not where it was this morning at ten. A shadow goes in a clockwise direction as the Earth rotates—that's why clocks go in that direction.

"Her shadow two hours after noon would be about the same length as her shadow two hours before noon," Karin added. "Since I knew both the distance and the direction it fell from where she's standing, it was obvious where to look."

18

Freeze Fall

It was late winter, and the temperature had just fallen after several mild days. To make the walk home from school even colder, it had rained earlier, and a chilly mist still hung in the air.

Tom and Evan glanced up at the flashing clock in front of the bank. It said "32°F, 0°C."

They stopped in a candy store for a snack and to warm up before they continued on their way home.

Their shoes splashed through puddles as they headed toward the railroad bridge. The bridge, several hundred yards long, had a narrow sidewalk next to train tracks, where the tracks crossed the river far below. It could get scary crossing the bridge when a train was on it. But the only way to avoid it was to take a different route that added ten minutes to the walk.

"I think we should go the long way," Evan said. "The bridge is probably icy."

"We haven't seen any ice. These sidewalks are just wet," Tom said.

A few moments later they were on the bridge. Tom's foot slipped on a patch of ice and he fell.

"I told you so," Evan said, teasing him.

"How did you know there would be ice here when there isn't ice anywhere else?" Tom asked as Evan helped him up.

"The Earth absorbs heat from the Sun and radiates that heat back out. Up until the bridge, there is ground under the sidewalks. The ground provides some insulation and keeps the sidewalks above the freezing point, even though the air temperature itself is at the freezing point," Evan said. "But underneath the bridge there is just cold air without any insulation, so the surface on the bridge freezes first."

Time for a Change

19

"That was a long flight!" Casey complained as the airplane touched down in California.

It was a five-hour flight from New York, and it was eight o'clock at night when they landed.

After getting their bags, Casey and his family took a rental car to their hotel.

They were going on vacation in Northern California. All of them were looking forward to going on a whale-watching boat the next day. Casey's father was hoping to play some golf. His mother was eager to drive along the coast. His little sister wanted to see sea otters.

By the time they checked into their hotel room, it was 9:30. It was Friday night and one of Casey's favorite things was to sleep in late on a Saturday morning. Often he would sleep as late as nine or ten o'clock in the morning.

"What time does the whale-watching boat leave?" he asked.

"Nine o'clock," his mother said. "We'll probably have to leave here around eight."

"Oh man, then I don't get to sleep in!" Casey said.

"Just sleep the way you usually do and it's no problem," she said.

"But we'll miss the boat," Casey said, setting the alarm clock.

"Really, you don't have to worry," his father said. Casey thought for a moment.

"Oh, I know what you're talking about," he said.

"What are you talking about?" his curious little sister asked.

"There's a three-hour time difference between the East and West coasts. It's three hours earlier out here than in the East, which means that when it is noon in New York, it's only nine o'clock in California," Casey said. "Our bodies are still on East Coast time. Even if I sleep in till ten in the morning according to the time my body thinks it is, that would still only be seven o'clock here in California. We have actually flown through all of the four main time zones in America today."

20

Stars in Their Eyes

Mr. Sakura was known for giving a lot of homework, and a lot of it was very tough. He also was known for having a sense of humor.

His assignment to the class was this: "Over the next week, at a time of your choosing, identify the star that looks the largest in the sky."

The day they turned in their answers, a group of friends gathered outside after school and talked about what they did.

"I used binoculars, but even then, no one star seemed bigger than any of the others," Xavier said. "So I just picked the North Star. I don't know if it's the biggest, but at least it's easy to find."

"I did some research on the Internet and found that Vega is a really bright star," Paul said. "I managed to find it one night. But I couldn't tell if it's the biggest star in the sky or not."

Bradley said, "I used a telescope I got as a little kid and looked at the constellation Orion—you know, the one that is supposed to look like a hunter wearing a belt. I picked one of the belt stars, Mintaka. I tried to measure it against the other ones. It looked a little bigger, but I don't really know."

"That's what you guys get for not looking closely enough," Nicholas said. "How could you miss it?"

"But we looked at the stars as closely as we could, without going to an observatory," Bradley said.

"You didn't look closely enough at the instructions," Nicholas said. "Remember, the instruction sheet said you could pick a star you see at any time you chose. It didn't say you had to pick a star at night. The star that looks the largest in the sky is right there," he said, pointing to the Sun. "The Sun is the only star in our solar system. It is the closest star to Earth and that's why it looks the biggest, but it turns out it is about average in size among all stars."

Rain or Shine

Sandrine's parents had let her use their digital camera at the class Halloween party. She went around taking pictures of the food, the decorations and everyone in their outfits.

Sandrine knew how to download pictures from the camera onto a computer, and over the weekend, she would email them to her friends.

"Sandrine, if you send out that picture of me stuffing my face with popcorn I will so kill you," Valencia said.

"Let's see! Let's see!" Lena said.

"Yeah, let's see!" Kathleen said. The four of them were the best of friends and always together.

Sandrine hit the button that showed all the pictures in the camera's memory. The earliest ones were from a game of a soccer team they all played on. But they showed only Sandrine, Kathleen and Valencia, not Lena. One picture of the three of them was especially good, with a clear sky and a rainbow in the background.

"Hey, where am I in these pictures?" Lena said, sounding a little jealous at being left out.

"Maybe you missed that game," Valencia said.

"I haven't missed a game since last spring," Lena said. "That day it rained before the game and I slipped and twisted my ankle during warm-ups and had to go home."

"Then this must be from that day," Sandrine said.

"Can't be. The sky is clear in this picture," Lena said.

"Sandrine's right," Valencia said. "The picture proves it. Don't you see how?"

"Rainbows only appear when sunlight hits water in the air at just the right angle," Valencia said. "So even though the sky had cleared out by the time this picture was taken, the rainbow proves that it had rained not long before."

Space Ship-Shape

"Space: the final frontier," Dixon said.

"To infinity and beyond!" Sarah yelled.

"Houston, we have a problem!" Ben shouted.

Most of what they knew about space they seemed to have learned from watching movies or television, Dixon's older brother Desmond thought. But Desmond had to hand it to them: They had written a pretty good space movie for a class assignment.

Desmond was there to video it, while the other three acted it out.

Sarah, Dixon and Ben had set up part of Sarah's family room to make it look like the inside of a spaceship. They had brought together various pieces of electronic equipment, had covered folding chairs and the wall behind them with aluminum foil and even had made futuristic-looking outfits.

The story showed them sitting strapped behind a control board full of knobs and lights, saving the Earth from a collision with an asteroid. They discovered the asteroid by looking at a computer screen, made warning calls to Earth on headsets, shot laser beams to destroy the asteroid and then poured glasses of orange juice to celebrate.

As they played the video back through the television, they congratulated each other on how well it came out.

"There's only one thing I'd change if I were you," Desmond said.

"What's that?" Dixon asked.

"Your story is accurate right up to the very end, where you poured the juice," Desmond said. "Astronauts don't pour drinks because there is only microgravity in outer space and the juice would fly all over the place. Why don't we re-shoot that last part and have you drinking out of juice boxes instead?"

Sight at Night

"Are you sure you know how to get there?" Ethan asked.

"Of course I'm sure," his older brother, Christopher, answered. "Have you ever known me to get lost driving?"

"No," Ethan said.

Ethan was about to add that Christopher hadn't been driving long, at least not without one of their parents in the car. In fact, this was the first time that Christopher had driven him without an adult in the front passenger's seat. Christopher had volunteered to drive because he wanted to practice driving at night, and there wouldn't be many cars on these roads to worry about.

They were on the way to a new ice rink where Ethan was going to learn hockey. Christopher had said he knew a shortcut. Unfortunately, it involved driving down dark roads out in the countryside where there were few houses and no street lights.

"It's pretty dark," Ethan said. "Are you sure you'll remember where to turn? All these side roads look alike."

"Don't worry," Christopher said.

"When was the last time you drove to the ice rink?" Ethan asked.

"Two weeks ago," Christopher said. "I could see it in the moonlight from the full Moon that night. It's not that cloudy. The Moon should come out any time now. As soon as it does, I'll recognize where to turn."

"In that case, I think we should call for directions," Ethan said.

"Why?" Christopher asked.

"The Moon has different phases depending on the position of the Sun, the Earth and the Moon. The total cycle lasts for about 29 1/2 days. That means that if there was a full Moon two weeks ago, we're right around a new Moon tonight," Ethan said. "Because the Moon has waned so much, there won't be any moonlight."

In Hot Water

Danielle and her family went to a hot-springs pool after a day that included ice skating on an outdoor rink and a horse-drawn sleigh ride through the snow. They were staying at a resort hotel that had hot springs.

They checked out the spot where the water was bubbling out from the ground, sending up wisps of steam. From there, the water flowed into a pool about the size of a small swimming pool. The sign said the water in that pool was 105° F (41° C). The water flowed down from there to another pool, where the temperature was 98° F (37° C).

They stayed in the 98° pool for about ten minutes and then went to the 105-degree pool. Danielle enjoyed sitting right where the water was flowing in from spring.

A man with a nametag that said "Charlie" came over to where the water was coming out of the ground and dipped a little glass container in the water. "What are you doing?" Danielle asked him.

"I'm just testing the chlorine level," he said.

Danielle had seen the lifeguards at the pool she belonged to back home test for chlorine.

But when the man walked away, she said to her father, "I think you ought to tell the people who are in charge here about that man. I bet he doesn't even work here. Maybe he's looking for a chance to steal somebody's wallet."

"What makes you think that?" her father asked.

"Since the water is coming right from the ground, there's no chlorine in it," Danielle said. "Anyone who worked here would know that."

"That's right," her father said. "Chlorine is found in water that has been treated for home use, and even more is added at swimming pools to kill bacteria in the water. I'll go talk to the manager."

25

Sands of Time

The Sun was already getting low in the sky over the Pacific Ocean when Joseph, his parents and his little brother, Fernando, went to the beach.

Some people were already packing up for the day, folding their chairs and umbrellas and picking up their coolers, but Joseph's parents had promised Fernando that they would go to the beach that day, the first of their vacation. They walked past a dark line in the sand where the beach sloped off toward the ocean, set up some blankets and got out the beach toys.

Joseph really didn't want to help Fernando build a sand castle, but his parents gave him a look that said he'd better do it if he was going to get that jet-ski ride he wanted. So Joseph helped out, taking a few steps to the water to get wet sand as they worked. By the time they finished, it was time to go back to their hotel, which was near the beach.

The next morning, Fernando said, "I wanna go see my castle!"

"Joseph, would you walk your brother down to the beach while your mother and I pack for our drive today?" their father asked in a tone of voice that wasn't a question.

Joseph sighed and walked Fernando toward where he thought they'd been the previous evening. But there was no sign of a sand castle.

"Some mean person knocked it down!" Fernando cried.

"No, that's not what happened," Joseph said.

"Then why isn't it here?" Fernando asked.

"Yesterday evening when we built the sand castle, it must have been low tide. There are two low tides and two high tides every day; they are caused by the Moon's gravitational pull. You can tell that by where the beach slopes off, and that line in the sand is where the high tide comes to," Joseph said. "We were down below that at the water's edge. During the night the tide came in and washed away our—I mean, your—sand castle."

Falling Foliage

26

One of the projects in Spanish class was a pen-pal arrangement with students from a school in Argentina. Each week the students wrote a letter using the Spanish they learned that told about themselves. One of their favorite things was describing where they lived, or what the plants and rocks were like there.

The students from the school in Argentina would write back using the English they were learning.

Soon the students from the two schools started sending pictures of themselves, their schools and their homes.

Finally they decided to plant a tree where they lived in honor of each other. By the end of May, each class raised enough money to buy a tree and have it planted.

When school started again in September, an envelope was waiting for the class. It contained a letter from Argentina that read: "Dear American friends: How are you? Here is a picture of the tree we planted in your name. We took this picture in July just after we planted it. Whenever we see it, we think of you. Please write back soon. Your friends in Argentina."

Their teacher pulled out a photograph of a leafless tree. Jordan groaned, "Oh, no, it died already!"

"No it didn't," said Noah.

"What makes you so sure?" Jordan asked.

"Argentina is in the Southern Hemisphere, so July is winter there—that's why their tree doesn't have any leaves," Noah said. "In a couple of months, I'm sure they'll send another picture showing the tree blooming in their springtime. Now let's go out and take a picture of the tree we planted before it loses its leaves and they think this one has died."

The Best-Laid Planets

On nice days like this one, the students in the after-school extended-day program could go out to the playground and fields. The counselors brought out boxes with supplies for games—jump ropes, chalk for drawing on the blacktop and a variety of balls. Sometimes they organized relay races and other games.

The catch was that students could go outside only after they finished their homework and one of the counselors checked their work.

Tekanya was one of the first to finish that day. She went outside but didn't feel like playing a game until her friend Tiara joined her. Instead, Tekanya lined up several balls to make a model of the solar system. The line pointed at the real Sun, just for the right effect.

She went back inside to her locker to get her jacket since it was colder than she thought, and then she met Tiara. By the time they went outside, most kids had finished their homework and also were outside. A few of them were starting a soccer game, some others were shooting baskets, a couple were throwing tennis balls and several were playing marbles.

"Oh, no, my solar system!" Tekanya said. Some of her "planets" had been taken.

"Oh, well, we might as well play something," she said to Tiara. "How about we get in the game with my Jupiter?"

"Which game is that?" Tiara asked.

"Basketball, of course," Tekanya said. "The basketball is the largest of these balls, and Jupiter is the largest of the planets."

28

That Snow Problem

It had been especially snowy for December. A storm early in the month dropped six inches (15 cm), then there was another storm with twice that much, and then a third with another eight inches (20 cm), and none of it had melted. The result was a number of snow days at school even before the upcoming ten-day winter break. But the teachers had promised a special activity on the last day of school before the break: a snow-sculpture contest. Each of the four grades in the middle school got one side of the building.

The fifth graders, who got the north side, built a traditional snowman, right down to the carrot for a nose. The sixth graders, who got the south side, built a snow castle. The seventh graders on the east side tried to make a dragon, although it ended up looking more like a dog, while the eighth graders on the west side made an igloo.

As they filed onto the bus in the afternoon sunshine and dodged the water dripping from the trees above the bus stop, students from each grade claimed theirs was the best.

"Ours is the most creative," said Thompson, a seventh grader.

"Yeah, well ours is the biggest," said Deanna, a sixth grader.

"Well, ours you can even crawl in," said Glenn, an eighth grader.

"All that may be true, but ours will be the one that lasts the longest," said Philip, a fifth grader.

"What do you mean by that?" Deanna asked.

"The Sun is finally starting to melt all this snow. That's why water is dripping from the trees," Philip said. "The Sun is in the southern sky and moves east to west—and it doesn't get very high in the sky in the winter. So my grade's snowman on the north side of the building will be in the shade while your dragon, castle and igloo are being melted."

29

Battle of the Bulge

Leo and Richard's families had been planning this vacation for a long time. They flew into Denver and then drove up from there into the mountains, where they had rented a cabin big enough for the two families. For the next four days, they would be mountain biking, hiking, fishing and just exploring the forest.

But first they had to unpack. The parents handled the clothes while Leo and Richard unpacked the food that Richard's family brought along in case they couldn't buy any nearby.

"What's this stuff?" Leo asked, taking out a container labeled "Soy Powder."

"My mother uses that because she needs more protein in her diet," Richard said. "You mix it with water."

"Are you sure it hasn't spoiled?"

"Nah, it's still good. It comes in those sealed containers, so it lasts a long time."

"Look at this." Leo pointed out that the plastic top of the container was bulging. "I read about this in health class. When canned food spoils, the bacteria give off a gas that makes the can bulge."

"Where was it packaged?" Richard asked.

"You mean when was it packaged?" Leo asked.

"No, where."

Leo looked at the label. "Miami."

"Then there's nothing to worry about," Richard said.

"What could where it was packaged have to do with it?" Leo asked.

"There might be a problem if it had been packaged at a high elevation," Richard said. "But it was sealed at a low elevation—Miami is right along the ocean at sea level—and we're at a high elevation now. Denver itself is a mile high*, and we're higher than even that. The higher the elevation, the lower the air pressure. The reason the lid is bulging is that the air pressure inside the container is greater than the air pressure outside of it."

*Denver is called the Mile High City because it sits at an elevation of 5,280 feet or 1.6 km.

30

Taking Directions

Just after arriving at school that morning, the sixth-grade class of Harrowgate Middle School climbed into a caravan of cars for a short drive to a nearby park.

The goal of the field trip was to make maps, using compasses and grid paper. They were divided into three-person groups, with each group starting from a different place. Samuel's father, who was one of the chaperones, drove him, Camille and Lexi to their starting place.

They got out of the car and laid the compass and paper on the hood, with Lexi on one side, Camille facing her on the other side and Samuel in between. Samuel's father stayed inside with the engine running to stay warm. Although it was a sunny day, it was chilly.

They chose Samuel to draw the map, Camille to count the steps and Lexi to use the compass.

"Okay, the directions say to make 50 steps equal to one line on the grid, and to start by going 100 steps south," Camille said. "Which way is south?"

Lexi squinted against the sunlight that was hitting the left side of her face as she looked down at the compass.

"The needle is pointing that way," Lexi said, pointing over Camille's shoulder. "Since a compass needle points north, south would be in the opposite direction. Behind me."

"That's not right," Samuel said.

Camille frowned at him. "Who do you expect us to believe, you or a compass?"

"It's morning, so the Sun is still in the east," Samuel said. "The sunlight is hitting the left side of your face, Lexi, so you must be facing roughly south, meaning Camille is to the south of you. Yes, a compass needle points north—unless something is interfering with it."

"I see what you mean," Camille said. "When a car's engine is running, its electrical system generates an electromagnetic field."

She moved the compass around on the car's hood. At different places, the needle pointed in different directions.

Lexi said, "Either we need to get away from the car or Samuel's dad needs to turn off the engine. Then we can get our bearings straight."

"I'll ask him to turn off the engine," Samuel said. "He's wasting energy and causing pollution by letting the car run like that."

Physical and Chemical Science

Grass Stained

"Now we have to start all over again," Alyce said. "And it's all your fault," she glared at her little brother.

"I didn't do anything!" Freddy protested.

Alyce had invited her friend Haley to come over early that Saturday morning. They were doing a project on migration. The previous weekend, they had watched geese flying above them in their V formations, honking as they flew south.

Alyce had read that hummingbirds migrate too, so after school the previous day, she had gone to the garden center and bought a glass feeder. She followed the instructions on assembling it exactly, and filled it to the top with a mixture of water and sugar, adding a couple of drops of red food coloring, and then hung it off a low branch of a tree in her backyard. She and Haley had planned to watch for hummingbirds every day for the next few weeks to see if the number changed as the weather got colder.

But when they came to the feeder, they saw that it was cracked and water had leaked out, leaving a red stain on the frosted grass.

"What makes you say Freddy broke it?" Haley asked.

Alyce said, "Because he was tagging along with me the whole time I was working on it. I just bet he was out here earlier playing with it and he dropped it and hung it back up."

"Did not!" Freddy hollered.

"Did too!" Alyce hollered back.

Haley said, "Actually, he's telling the truth. Can you see why?"

"The water inside the feeder is what cracked the glass," Haley said. "You filled it to the top last night, right? This morning, there's frost on the grass. That means it got below freezing last night. And when water freezes, it expands. Enough of it has melted now to leak out, but I bet if we look closely, we'll see that most of the water inside is still frozen."

Faded Memory

Javier and the others from his class gathered in the school auditorium along with many adults. It had turned into a town holiday.

Long ago, students at the school had made a time capsule out of a large metal box and sealed it, to be opened exactly 100 years from that date. The day had arrived.

According to a newspaper story from the time that they had read in class, the most valuable thing in the box was a painting. It was a battle scene done by a famous artist who lived in the town as a child and who donated the painting to the school. Painted copies of it were in museums everywhere, but this was the original, which was sealed up not long after it was first painted, and was now worth a lot of money.

Several people were needed to carry the large box, which had a fancy inscription on the outside. "To the School Children of the 21st Century," it said.

The band played as the box was opened. Everyone stretched to see. Out came a pair of shoes with laces like those on ice skates. There were also a couple of home-made dolls and some tops, checkers and cards.

Then several men pulled out something very carefully. It was the painting.

Everyone took turns looking at it closely. "Too bad the colors faded so much in all that time it was sealed away," said Theo, who was in front of Javier.

"Too bad somebody opened the time capsule before now, stole the original painting and substituted a copy," Javier said.

"What makes you say that?" Theo asked.

"That painting must be one of the copies," Javier told Theo. "Paint only fades from years of being exposed to light, which wouldn't happen inside a metal box. Someone must have unsealed the box, switched the paintings and then resealed it."

Taken With a Grain of Salt

One evening, the campers cooked their own meals with their cooking kits over open fires outside the dining hall. Then, they brought the food inside where the tables were set up for dinner as usual, and desserts were on a side table.

Mark should have known better than to get up from the table to get a dessert without taking his glass of water along, because when he got back to the table, he saw that the glass had been moved. He couldn't quite be sure, but he thought the salt shaker had been moved too. And a couple of the guys looked like they were trying hard not to laugh.

"Did you guys put salt in my water?" Mark asked.

"There's only one way to find out," Breon said, picking up the glass and handing it to him. "Take a nice deep drink."

"I bet I can find out without tasting even a drop of it," Mark said. "Without anyone else tasting it either. And without anyone telling me."

"What do you want to bet?" Breon responded.

"Chores for the rest of the week," Mark said. "If I win, you do mine. If you win, I do yours."

"You're on," Breon said. "How are you going to prove it?"

"I'll take the glass out to the campfire, pour the water into my cooking pan and let the water boil off," Mark said. "If there's salt in the water, it's in solution now and we can't see it, but once I remove the water by boiling it off, any salt will stay behind in the pan."

Double Dealing

Sherry and Marlena were identical twins, but usually it wasn't too hard to tell them apart. Unlike some twins, they didn't wear the same kinds of clothes, and they wore different hairstyles.

But for the ballet class's performance of "The Nutcracker," the teacher, Miss Jody, had put them in identical costumes and pulled their hair up into identical buns to be Snowflake Princesses.

Miss Jody had decorated their faces with a shiny plastic snowflake, one on Sherry's right cheek and one on Marlena's left cheek, so that when they faced each other at the end of the dance, the light from the spotlight glittered back into the audience. They had gotten a big round of applause.

Afterward, while the girls were removing their makeup and standing in front of the dressing room mirrors, Blaise came up from behind. The face that reflected back at her had a flake on the left side.

"Nice dancing, Marlena," she said.

"Thanks. You did your Sugarplum Fairy dance very well, Blaise. But I'm Sherry. Can't you tell us apart?"

"Quit joking, Marlena."

"I'm not joking," the girl said.

"Yes you are," Blaise said. But she was beginning to wonder. It was Marlena who had the snowflake on her left cheek, she had been sure of that. Up to now.

"Why would I pretend to be Marlena? I'm much better looking," the girl laughed, her back still to Blaise. "Or am I Marlena? Can you tell?"

"I see now," Blaise said. "When I look at your reflection coming back at me in the mirror, the flake is on the left side as I see it, but of course the mirror reverses everything. So the flake actually is on your right cheek, so you really are Sherry."

Cabin Fever

"Just the way Mother Nature wants us to sleep in the summer," the counselor said when she showed the friends their cabins, which didn't have air conditioning, or even fans.

Even though she was in the same grade as most of her friends, Grace was in a different cabin because she was younger. So she went off to her cabin while Katya, Nina and Chloe settled into their cabin. Each cabin had six sets of bunk beds plus a single bed for the counselor.

The next morning, in the bathroom building the cabins shared, the girls talked excitedly about the day ahead. Katya's face looked red and she kept wiping herself with a wet towel, while Nina and Chloe brushed their hair.

"Did you guys get any sleep?" Grace asked. "Our counselor turned off the lights at exactly ten o'clock and there was no talking after that. So I slept fine."

"So did I," Nina said.

"Me too," said Chloe.

"Not me," Katya said. "I was so hot that I just stared at the ceiling all night!"

"You might want to ask for a different bunk," Grace said.

"What good would that do?" Katya asked. "They're all the same."

"See if someone who's on a bottom bunk and who doesn't mind heat so much will switch with you," Grace said. "If you were staring at the ceiling, obviously you were in a top bunk. Hot air rises, so the top bunks are hotter."

Pumpkin Patch

"Where's Linus? We have the Great Pumpkin," Belinda said.

Madison laughed. It was Halloween, and all the neighbors around the cul-de-sac were going in on a contest to see who carved the best pumpkin. The prize was a gift certificate to the video store.

She and Belinda had carved a pumpkin with the face of a witch and then used colored paper to cover the openings so that the light from the candle inside would make the face glow green. They lit the candle, put the top back on the pumpkin and went out trick-or-treating

As they went from house to house, they looked over the other entries for the contest. Carly had done a nice carving of a ghost, and Peter had used an odd-shaped pumpkin to make a funny-looking frog. They came to Sam's house just as he was setting out his pumpkin.

"This is the winner right here," Sam said, in a not-too-friendly voice. Madison had to admit, he'd done a good job of carving a haunted house, but she still knew her and Belinda's pumpkin was better.

"Watch out for him," Belinda said as they went to the next house. "He'll probably smash the other pumpkins just so he can win."

After they made a lap of the neighborhood, they returned to Madison's house to drop off the candy before everyone would meet for the winner to be announced. Their pumpkin was not smashed, but the candle was out, so it didn't look like anything special.

"I know who's to blame," said Madison.

"Who?" Belinda asked.

"It's our fault," Madison said. "The candle went out on its own. When we covered up the holes with the paper and put the lid on, we cut off the oxygen supply. Fire needs oxygen to keep going. Looks like Sam's going to be the winner. Maybe he'll invite us to watch the movie he gets with that gift certificate."

Thirst for Knowledge

"Man, I need a cold drink!" Ryan said.

It was one of those steamy, sticky days. Ryan and his friend Jonas had just finished a summer-league baseball game and were trotting off the field.

Parents took turns serving the snacks after the game. Before the last inning, the players noticed Jonas's father pouring lemonade into plastic cups and lining them up on the bottom row of the bleachers.

The inning turned out to be a long one, though. The other team scored several runs, pinch-hitters were sent in and there were two changes of pitchers before Ryan and Jonas's team won. The drinks sat out in the hot sun a long time—so long that some of the parents drank a couple, and Jonas's father needed to pour more from the plastic jug that he kept in an ice-filled cooler. When the players got off the field, the freshly poured drinks were mixed in with the ones that had been sitting out in the heat.

Jonas looked at the line of cups, searching for a cold one. He passed up one that was wet on the outside, even though it had more lemonade than the others.

"Looks like Dad spilled a little when he was pouring that one," he said. "I'll take a dry cup. That way my hands won't get all sticky."

"I'd rather have the wet cup," Ryan said.

"Why?" Jonas asked.

"The cold liquid inside the cups caused water vapor in the air to condense on the outside of the cups," Ryan said. "So the cups with water on the outside have cold liquid in them. The cups that are dry on the outside have been sitting out in the sun long enough for the liquid to warm up, and the water that had condensed on them evaporated off. And my hands won't get sticky from a cold cup because that's condensation on the outside, not lemonade."

Gem Jam

"My parents will kill me! They will absolutely kill me!"

From the look on Ruby's face as she said that, Carmen didn't have to ask what had happened.

Carmen had just stepped out of the room to call her parents and ask them to pick her up from Ruby's birthday party. Most of the others had left. The group was down to just four close friends—Ruby, Carmen, Victoria and Triena—sitting around Ruby's kitchen table, picking at the cake and finishing their drinks—water for Carmen, Victoria and Triena, the last of the cherry punch for Ruby.

The gifts were stacked in a neat pile in the corner—most of them, that is. The most valuable present, by far, had not come from one of the guests. Ruby's parents had given her a gemstone to match her name. Ruby had been showing it around and debating whether to have it mounted on a ring or in a necklace when she realized it was missing.

"You lost the ruby?" Carmen asked after she returned to the kitchen.

"We were passing it around, and then I guess I got distracted and, well . . . I don't know what happened. We've been searching all over for it since you went out," Ruby said.

The way she said it carried just a hint of suspicion. Could Victoria or Triena have stolen it?

The others seemed to catch the implication, too. "If you want, you can search me," Victoria said. Triena nodded in agreement.

"No need for that," Carmen said, looking at the table. "I have an idea where it could be."

"Where?" Ruby asked.

Carmen asked Ruby to get a strainer. She poured Ruby's glass of cherry punch into it. The strainer caught the gem as the liquid drained away into the sink.

"That was the most likely place to lose a red stone in this room—in red liquid. Both the liquid and the stone are absorbing the same colors from the light spectrum," Carmen said. "Ruby, you should hurry up and get it mounted before you lose it again."

Hearing Aide

The after-school course on manners was a big hit with the parents, although most of the kids had to be dragged to it.

Today's lesson was on table manners. Margo, Amir, Hannah and Scott were seated at a table that had been set up in a classroom, alternating boys and girls. First, the instructor, Mrs. Walz, taught them how to set a table, and what each spoon, fork and knife was for. Then they learned about folding a napkin into a triangle and placing it on their laps and putting the bread plate on the left and the drinking glass on the right.

Margo's job was to pour water for everyone. She filled Amir's crystal glass, then Hannah's. But that used up all the water in the pitcher, so she couldn't put any in her glass or Scott's. Hannah drank half of her water, realized she wasn't supposed to drink before everyone had been served, and then put down her glass.

Margo and Mrs. Walz walked out to the water fountain to refill the pitcher. While they were out there, they heard a high-pitched sound of silverware clinking against a glass.

"Yes, good crystal like these glasses does make a sound when you tap it like that," Mrs. Walz said when she and Margo walked back into the room. "But it's not proper, not unless you're calling for attention to make a toast. Now, who did it?"

"It was Scott. But to prove it, I'll have to do the same thing," Margo said. She took a fork and tapped each of the glasses. "When you tap a glass it vibrates to make a sound, but water in the glass slows the vibrations. Amir's glass makes a low-pitched sound because it's full of water," she said. "Hannah's makes a medium-pitched sound because it's half full. Scott's glass makes the high pitch we heard because it's empty."

Too Hot to Handle

Rachel's little sister Savannah was having her fourth birthday party on a sunny September day that wasn't too hot. Savannah had invited everyone from her preschool class. More than a dozen of them were in her backyard, playing tag, swinging on the swing and bouncing on the moon bounce that Rachel's parents had rented.

It was almost time to eat and to open the presents. But Rachel's mother had planned an activity to calm them down first: making wax flowers from kits.

Rachel helped the younger children with the project. Eventually, they lined up a series of wax flower pots along the railing of the deck.

"I'm going to make sure no bees get mine," Savannah said, and she put a drinking glass over hers. They all went inside for cake, ice cream and presents, and it was a while before they returned outside.

The flowers were all as they had left them, except for Savannah's. "Mine melted!" she cried.

"My goodness, it did," her mother said. "But it's not that hot out here—none of the others melted. I wonder what happened."

"The greenhouse effect happened," Rachel said. "Covering Savannah's wax flower with the glass trapped the air inside. That air got hotter and hotter as the sunshine came through the glass and heated the air inside. The other flowers didn't melt because the air kept circulating around them. How about if I help you make another one, Savannah?"

41

Storm Warning

One thing the campers had to watch out for in the summer was thunderstorms. Storms could rise up quickly in the west in the afternoon, and sometimes they caught hikers by surprise.

Alicia, Shandiz, Leslie and their counselor Sabrina had hiked a long distance to the east from camp. They stopped to rest at a shelter and saw dark clouds forming far off in the distance, beyond the camp.

Sabrina took out a walkie-talkie and called to the camp.

"There's a storm coming in," said the camp director on the other end. "The radio says it will get here in 20 minutes. Are you going to try to come back before it hits?"

"I don't know how far away we are," Sabrina said. "It takes us about 20 minutes to walk a mile or about 1.6 km."

Just then the girls heard the sound of thunder coming through the walkie-talkie.

Alicia started counting. "One, two, three, four, five, six, seven, eight, nine, ten . . ." Then she heard thunder overhead.

"What do you think? Should we go back or should we stay in this shelter and wait for the storm to pass?" Sabrina asked.

"We should stay here," answered Alicia.

"Why?" Sabrina asked.

"Sound travels about a mile, or about 1.6 km, through the air in five seconds," Alicia said. "We heard the thunder at the camp right away through the walkie-talkie because that sends electrical signals, which are much faster. It was ten seconds from the time the thunder passed over the camp until the sound got here. That means we're about two miles, or 3.2 km, away from the camp. Taking 20 minutes to walk a mile means we would get to the camp in 40 minutes. The storm will be there in about 20 minutes. We wouldn't make it there before the storm hits."

Fingering the Culprit

42

Molly could hear the giggling as she came back from the supply room with more paper.

She was the volunteer helper in the kindergarten class, which meant that once a week during "specials" period, rather than go to art or music, she went to the kindergarten room to help the teachers there. Molly wanted to be a teacher someday and thought this would be a good learning experience.

Among the things she was learning was that kindergarteners like to play practical jokes. Sometimes they would slip things in her backpack. Other times they would put tape on her clothes.

Allie, DayShawn, Tyler and Henry were giggling as Molly returned. Molly had told them to finger-paint an outdoor scene using water paints. Allie was drawing a big Sun in the corner, DayShawn was making the grass and Tyler was doing the sky. Henry was coming back from the sink.

One of them had done a red finger-paint drawing of a girl with a big frown on her face and underneath it had written "Molly." All of them were pretending that they didn't know anything about it.

"Which of you should I thank for this beautiful picture of me?" Molly said, playing along. "Show me your hands."

Each of them held up their hands. Allie's fingertips were yellow, although she had orange between some of her fingers. DayShawn's fingers were green and Tyler's blue. Henry's hands were clean.

"Thanks for showing me who made it," Molly said.

"How do you know?" Tyler asked.

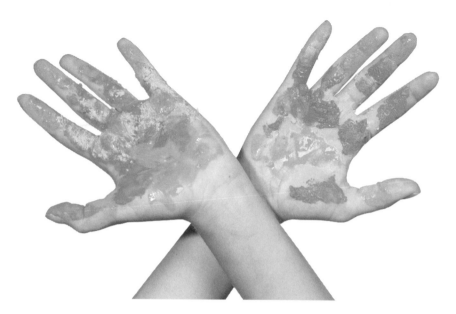

Molly said, "You get orange when you mix yellow and red, which is why Allie's fingers had orange. The yellow from the Sun she's doing now mixed with the red from the drawing of the girl she did while I was getting the paper. Actually, I like the drawing. Let's change that frown to a smile and I'll take it home to put on my refrigerator."

Slow Burn

It was a chilly evening, with a cool breeze blowing off the lake. It had rained earlier, but now the sky was clear and full of stars. The girls huddled around the campfire, singing silly songs, telling jokes and talking about the hike coming up the next day.

They decided it was time to roast marshmallows. Patti ran back into her tent to get a bag, while Zoe rounded up some thin sticks. Gretchen picked up some firewood from the pile she had gathered earlier and laid a few pieces across the fire.

For a while, though, the new wood just smoldered, with smoke drifting up from it, but no flames.

"Are you sure that's not petrified wood you put in there, Gretchen?" Fernanda asked.

"Ha, ha," Gretchen said.

"When did you get it?" Logan asked.

"Just before we made the fire," Gretchen responded.

As they started roasting marshmallows, a loud crack came from the fire. Everybody jumped back.

"Okay, who's the joker with the firecrackers?" Zoe demanded.

Nobody answered.

"Whoever did it, it's not funny," she said. "Come on, who did it?"

"The wood must have gotten wet during the rain earlier today," Patti said. "That's why it didn't catch fire right away. The water inside the wood got hot enough to make steam, and the pressure of the steam broke the wood open and made that cracking sound. It's the same thing that happens when you pop popcorn."

It Works Like Magic

"I am William the Great!"

William was on the stage at the beginning of the talent show. Later on there would be singing, dancing, a gymnast, piano players, instrumental duets and a comedy routine. But William was on stage first, dressed as a magician in a long black cape and a top hat. He did a few card tricks, then asked for volunteers to come onto the stage. Stacie was one of them.

William showed the volunteers a piece of white rope a couple of feet long and told them to examine it closely. Stacie twisted it, tied a knot and then untied it. It was just an ordinary piece of loose rope.

William handed them some markers. "Write anything you want on it so when you see it later, you'll know it is the same rope," he said.

William left the stage as the other acts came out. It was more than an hour later before he came back on stage. "And now for the grand finale!" he said. He pulled a rope from under his cape. It was the same rope, except that when he held it out in front of him with one hand, it was stiff. He waved it around like a wand.

Everyone clapped while he put the rope away in a case. He walked down the aisle, shaking people's hands, including Stacie's best friend, Abby.

"He must get nervous on stage," Abby said. "His hand was so wet and cold."

"It was a cool trick, but I think I know how he did it," Stacie said.

"How?" asked Abby.

Stacie said, "While the other acts were on stage, William must have soaked the rope in water and then frozen it in the cafeteria freezer. At the end of the show he brought it back and held it out. That's why his hand was wet and cold. Didn't you notice that he didn't let people touch the rope the second time?"

Hide and Seek

It had snowed the previous evening, and the schools were closed. Rebecca's father had gone to work anyway. Her mother was staying home, although she needed to work on the computer all day. Rebecca would be babysitting her younger sister Maia—and also Maia's friends from up the street, Erica, Elena and Ashley, who would be coming to play.

The younger girls went outside to play in the snow. Rebecca had to go with them to keep an eye on them. She stood shivering in the cold air. Rebecca didn't like the cold, and she especially didn't like getting wet from the snow.

Soon the younger girls decided to play hide and seek. Erica, Elena and Ashley would hide and Maia would try to find them. Rebecca played along, turning her back and closing her eyes along with Maia and counting slowly to 20.

"Let's see, where could they be?" Rebecca said, although she knew exactly where they had to be.

She whispered to Maia, "If I tell you where they are, will you promise to convince them to come inside?"

"Well, it looks like some snow has been knocked off the azalea bushes and there are footprints leading to the porch. But how do you know where the last one is?" Maia asked.

"She's in the playhouse," said Rebecca.

"Are you sure? How can you tell with the window all fogged up?" wondered Maia.

Page 110

"It's because the window is fogged up that I know someone is in there. The only way the playhouse window would fog up in this weather is from someone's breath," Rebecca said. "Cold air is very dry, so the fog is caused by the moisture in her breath condensing on the glass. She must be hiding right below the window so she can peek out at us. Now let's all go inside for some hot chocolate. I'm freezing!"

General Science

Needing a Lift

"Hey, watch out!" Karl said.

"Oops, sorry!" Barry said.

It was Earth Day, and as part of their project, they were planting trees at the elementary-school playground. Karl and Barry each had taken one handle of a wheelbarrow. In the wheelbarrow was a tree, its roots protected by a heavy cloth sack full of dirt. As they crossed the playground toward the holes that had already been dug for the trees, they struggled to control the wheelbarrow because of the weight.

As they got near the see-saw, Barry's hand had slipped and he let go of his handle. The wheelbarrow tipped over and the tree slid out onto the ground.

The two of them tried to pick it up, but it was too heavy.

Alejandro and DeWayne came to help, but even the four of them couldn't lift the tree. "We'd better stop before we hurt ourselves," Alejandro said.

"How about if we push it?" DeWayne suggested.

They did manage to scoot it across the ground a little.

"That won't work. Even if we could push it all the way to the hole, the sack would tear and we'd ruin the roots," Barry said.

"I have an idea," Karl said.

"Let's hear it," Barry said.

"A see-saw is a lever," Karl said. "Let's adjust it so the side next to the tree is the short end. Then we'll push the root ball onto that end. Alejandro and DeWayne, you push down on the long end, I'll hold the tree steady and Barry can move the wheelbarrow underneath it." In a few moments, the tree was back in the wheelbarrow and on its way to being planted.

Water, Water Everywhere

"Isn't that tree looking really pretty already?" Bridget said to her little sister Jessalyn, as they walked out onto the back porch.

Just then, Bridget heard a car door slam in the front of the house. "That would be Zane leaving," she said to herself. Their older brother was a travel soccer player, and would be gone until late that evening.

Even though it was only spring, it was already really sunny and hot. "I'm kind of worried about the tree," Jessalyn told Bridget. "It looks a little droopy."

They hadn't expected such hot weather so soon when they planted the tree the day before. Earlier, they called the nursery to ask what to do, and the woman there told them to water the tree for ten minutes in the morning and in the afternoon. But don't water it too much, she said.

Bridget did the morning watering, and Zane was supposed to do the afternoon watering just before he left. But he was running late as usual, and they weren't sure if he had done it.

Bridget and Jessalyn walked up the slope of the yard to the tree. The hose was connected to the spigot at the house, and stretched across the yard to the tree. But they couldn't tell from looking at the tree if it had been watered.

"If he didn't water it, it needs water now," Jessalyn said. "But if he did water it, we shouldn't give it any more. What should we do?"

Bridget asked Jessalyn to turn on the spigot. The water that came out of the hose was warm.

"That proves that Zane didn't water the tree," Bridget said. "Water has been in the hose since I watered the tree this morning, and it warmed up in the sun. The water didn't run out because the hose was lying on a slope and the spigot was turned off at the low end. If he had watered the tree just a few minutes ago, the water in the hose would still be cool, the way it is when it comes out of the spigot."

She put the hose back at the base of the tree to water it, and reminded herself that Zane owed her a favor.

48

Shocking Surprise

Lelia and Deejay were spending the afternoon at Davonne's house working on a group science project—building models of iron atoms. After hunching over Styrofoam protons, neutrons and electrons for a while, they decided to take a break. Davonne went out onto the deck and closed the screen door behind her.

The CD that had been playing on the boom box on the counter stopped. Her friends didn't like the music and had been kidding her about it. One of them must have turned it off.

Behind her, one of her friends must have gone into the living room, because Davonne heard someone talking to her younger brother, Gerald, who was playing on the carpet there. Her other friend must have gone into the dining room because she heard footsteps on its hardwood floor. But Davonne didn't know who went where because they were behind her.

When they all returned to the kitchen table a few minutes later, Lelia went to the refrigerator for a glass of water and quickly pulled her hand back when she touched the metal door handle. "Shocking," Deejay said, opening the refrigerator for her.

As Davonne went to turn the CD back on, she discovered that it was gone. She looked through to the living room and saw Gerald spinning it on his finger.

"Gerald!" she yelled. "Quit taking my stuff!"

"I didn't take it!" Gerald yelled back.

Davonne turned to her friends. "Okay, one of you gave it to him. And I know which one."

"Then tell us," Deejay said.

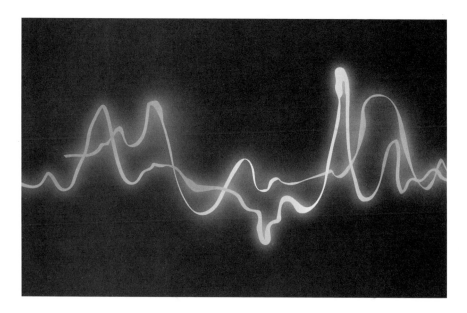

"I get shocks all the time around here," Davonne said. "But only after being in the living room and walking on the carpet in there. Static electricity doesn't build up when you walk on wood. Lelia got shocked and Deejay didn't when you both touched the metal handle of the refrigerator door. That means Lelia was the one who went into the living room and gave the CD to Gerald."

49

Stuck With the Mud

At Grady and Jim's school, there was a courtyard enclosed by classrooms on all sides. There were flower beds, berry bushes, trees with bird houses and even a little pond with lily pads, frogs and turtles. A couple of times a year, there was a workday during each science class to fertilize the plants, cut off dead branches and otherwise keep the courtyard in shape. This was one of those days, a cloudy, cool, damp day in the fall.

Jim and Grady had just finished tying back some branches with strong string when the teacher, Mr. Burke, assigned them another chore. He handed them a cloth bag and a shovel.

"Dig a little soil from the edge of the pond, dry it out, and bring it into the classroom. We're going to test it for bacteria in a few minutes," he said.

"Dry it out?" Grady asked.

"Damp is okay. Just dry enough so it doesn't drip. The custodian will be upset if we get mud on the floor," Mr. Burke said as he left them.

Grady held the bag while Jim shoveled in some gooey dirt, then laid the bag on the ground. Some water oozed out, but what was left was still very wet. "Man, it will take forever for this to dry out. And it's almost time to go back inside," Grady said.

"All we have to do is speed up the process," Jim said.

"How?" Grady asked. "If you expect me to squeeze that glop out, you're nuts."

"Stand back," Jim said. He used the string to tie the cloth bag shut and to swing the bag in circles. Water came flying out of the bag. "It's just a matter of using centrifugal force," Jim said. "When the bag is spun in a circle, the water is free to move through the bag while the dirt is held inside and is pressed against the inside of the bag. So I knew it would squeeze the water out, leaving only damp dirt inside.

"By the way," he added, "centrifugal force is what's called a 'pseudo' force, compared with 'real' forces like gravity or magnetism that have external causes. Centrifugal force exists here because the string is keeping the bag from continuing in a straight line, which inertia otherwise would make the bag follow once it was set in motion. The string is causing the bag and the dirt inside to constantly change direction by spinning the bag in a circle. The bag doesn't restrict the water, so the inertia of the water – which keeps it moving in one direction – makes the water fly out of the bag."

Valentine Vexation

The school student council was putting up decorations for the Valentine's Day party later that day in the multi-purpose room. Elinor came into the room a bit late. As council president, she had been talking with the principal about some of the details.

Her friends were sitting around a table, blowing up balloons and snacking on the food some parents had brought. Soo was sipping fruit punch, Jada had a cupcake, Olivia was munching on carrot sticks and Cimone was eating a peanut-butter sandwich. As each girl blew up a balloon, she used a marker to decorate it.

When they finished, Soo headed off to a corner to put up pink streamers while Cimone started to arrange flowers on the tabletops. Elinor, Jada and Olivia gathered up some red, pink and white balloons and started to tape them onto the walls.

As she was getting ready to tape up one of the balloons, Elinor saw that a message had been written on it: "Elinor likes Gary."

"Who did this?" Elinor called out.

"That's for us to know and you to find out," Olivia said.

"I will find out," Elinor said, taking the balloon out into the hallway.

She soon returned and said, "Okay, Cimone, confess. I know you did it."

"How do you know?" Jada asked.

"In the hallway, I unknotted the balloon and let the air out slowly, sniffing it as it came out," Elinor said. "I knew the air in the balloon would smell like anything that was on the breath of the person who blew it up. The air smelled like peanut butter."

Language Barrier

It was spring break and it was time for the trip they had been waiting for all year.

At the start of the school year, their French teacher, Madame Duval—everyone just called her "Madame"—had said the best way to learn about a country and its language was to go there. So the students saved all year to get enough money for a trip to France.

The plane, part of a French airline company, had left New York the previous evening and had flown all night on its way to Paris. Now the sunlight was starting to come in through the airplane windows. Most of the students and the parents who came along—along with Madame herself—were still asleep. But Amanda and Cara were awake, along with some of the other passengers.

The flight attendant started making announcements. They could tell right away that they were over France now, because she was speaking in French, not the English she had used when they took off.

Amanda and Cara couldn't understand everything she was saying, but they knew enough French to know she was saying they would be landing soon.

"She's talking about the weather today in Paris," said Amanda. "I heard her say 'il fait vingt-cinq degrés.' That means 'it is 25 degrees.' I didn't think it would be that cold in Paris this time of year. I hope I brought warm enough clothes."

Cara thought for a moment. "I don't think I'll wear a coat at all today," she said.

"But won't you freeze?" Amanda asked.

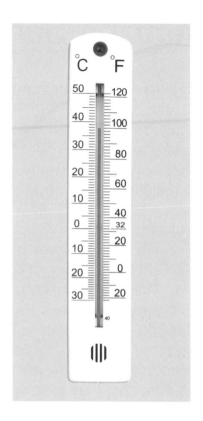

"In Europe, temperatures are in Celsius, not Fahrenheit," Cara said. "I did the conversion like they taught us in science class."

"Uh, right," Amanda said. "Can you refresh my memory on that?"

"You double the Celsius number, subtract one-tenth of the result, then add 32," Cara said. "Twenty-five times two is 50, and one-tenth of that is five. Fifty minus five is 45, and adding 32 makes 77. So 25° C is 77° F. A nice, warm spring day in Paris. What could be better?"

Powerful Argument

Jeremy, Vishal and Aiden met in the extended-day room before school one day to assemble the project they'd all been working on. It was a model of a city, showing how services such as water and electricity are delivered. The model had miniature businesses and homes along streets, with model-railroad telephone poles strung with thread to represent power lines, and air hoses from a fish tank to represent water lines.

They had put most of it together after school the day before when they realized they had forgotten to make a power plant. Aiden had volunteered to do that, and this morning he brought in a clay model of a building to use as the power plant for the finishing touch.

"You know, this doesn't look much like a power plant," Vishal said, examining it. "It's missing something . . . I know, it has no smokestacks!"

"So what?" Aiden said.

"Power plants burn fuel to generate electricity. You burn coal, you need a smokestack. You burn oil, you need a smokestack," Vishal said.

"Well, it's too late," Aiden said. "I didn't bring any more clay with me, and we have to turn this in during first period."

"There goes our grade," Vishal grumbled.

"Take it easy. I know how to fix this," Jeremy said, walking toward the cafeteria. He returned with some aluminum foil.

"What are you going to do with that?" Aiden asked.

Jeremy folded the foil so it would fit on top of the roof of the model power plant. "Now it's a solar power plant, which means it gets energy from the Sun. Nothing gets burned, so no smoke is made, and no smokestack is needed."

Nothing to Sneeze At

Miss Crater had been a teacher for so long at the school that she had taught the parents of some of her current pupils. They had many stories about her, including that she was the first teacher in the school to replace her blackboard with a whiteboard, because after many years of sneezing all day, she finally realized she had an allergy problem.

When she retired, the parents organized a big party for her. They decorated her classroom and held the party on a Saturday afternoon so that more people could come.

Of course, that meant that some of her students had to go there directly from their Saturday activities. Trent and Gabby were still in their soccer uniforms, Michelle was in a judo outfit, Shannon in horse-riding boots, T.J. in baseball cleats and Natalie in her gymnastics warm-ups. Nina had come from piano lessons, Isabelle from dance class, Jason from the skateboarding park.

Miss Crater said again and again how happy and thankful she was as she opened the presents the students had brought in with them. She picked up a heavy large box, shook it, sneezed and then laughed.

"I don't have to look at the card to know who this one is from because it reminds me of someone's activity," she said.

"Who is it from?" several people asked.

"Natalie, of course," Miss Crater said.

"You're right, it's from me," Natalie said. "Sorry, I forgot to wash the gymnastic chalk off my hands before I came. I know you're allergic to chalk dust. I hope you enjoy the present anyway."

Lights Out

Suddenly, the metal popcorn bowl fell to the hardwood floor and made a crashing sound that woke Nicole's parents.

Kayla, Nicole, Charlotte and Kendall were having a sleepover at Nicole's house. They had eaten way too much popcorn, called friends and watched a movie. Nicole's parents had checked on them at 10:30, let the four friends know that they needed rest and requested that they turn off the lights and get quiet in half an hour. Nicole and her friends had agreed.

Now, after 11, Nicole's mother was standing at the top of the steps in her night robe, the light from the hallway shining behind her.

"Did you turn the lights out like you agreed?" she asked.

"Sure, don't you see how dark it is in here?" Nicole replied.

"It's dark now, but maybe you turned off the lights after the bowl fell because you knew I'd be coming down," her mother said.

"No, really, Mom. The lights were out," Nicole said. "I just knocked over the bowl when I got up to get another pillow. I know you want to trust our agreements. Would it help if I could show you that the lights have been out for a while?"

"Sure, how?" her mother asked.

Nicole said to her mother, "Come down here and feel the light bulbs. These lights all get hot when they're on."

Nicole's mother felt the light bulbs and all of them were cool. "I'm glad that I can trust you," she told Nicole. "Now, let's get back to sleep."

Salad Days

Devin's family was hosting the party at the end of the spring basketball season. The players, coaches, parents, brothers and sisters were all celebrating winning the championship playoffs.

It was a potluck party. Everyone had brought something to eat. There was barbecued chicken, potato wedges, chips, fruit salad, garden salad and ice cream. There were cups lined up on a picnic table for people to help themselves to the drinks of soda, bottled water and punch.

Devin's mother was filling bowls with salad, while his father was at the grill, finishing cooking the chicken. "The food's ready," his father finally announced.

Everyone formed a line, taking a plate and filling it with food. Devin was helping his mother pass out the salad bowls.

"What kind of salad is it?" one of the players, Avery, asked.

"Looks like a regular salad, with lettuce and carrots and olives," she said.

"Is there oil and vinegar dressing on it?" Avery asked. "I really don't like that."

"I don't know," she said. "Jackson's mother dropped this off but she had to leave."

"Jackson, did your mother put oil and vinegar dressing on this salad?" Avery asked him.

"I don't know," Jackson said. "I guess you'll just have to taste it to find out."

"I know a better way. Allow me to demonstrate," Devin said, theatrically going to the drinks table.

"What are you doing?" Avery asked.

"I'll just put a little of that salad in a cup of water," Devin said. "Oil and water don't mix. If there's oil on the salad, it will float to the top." Soon they saw little beads of oil on the water.

"I'll just eat the fruit salad instead," Avery said.

Bird Watching

"It's one o'clock. Time for my shift," Mike said as he opened the gate into Garreth's backyard.

For science class, Mike and Garreth were counting how many birds came to a feeder in two-hour time spans in the morning, mid-day and evening. That Saturday morning, they set up a bird feeder at Garreth's house, which was next door to Mike's, and sat in his yard from eight o'clock to ten, counting the birds.

But there wasn't enough to do for two people, so they decided that for the other two periods, each would take one hour.

Mike sat down in the chair next to Garreth and looked at the fizzing drink on the ground next to him. Garreth noticed Mike eyeing it and said, "I opened that thing at noon when I started and I've been sitting here with it the whole time and forgot to drink it. Do you want me to go inside and get you one?"

"No, thanks. How did the bird watching go?" Mike asked.

Garreth showed him the sheet. There were hardly any marks on it. "Well, you can see, not many birds came for lunch."

Mike said, "You would have seen more if you had been sitting here the whole time like you say you were."

"What makes you think I wasn't?" Garreth asked.

"If you opened that soda an hour ago at noon like you said, it would have gone flat by now," Mike said. "But it's still fizzing, so you must have just opened it. That meant you went in the house, and probably not just to get a soda. Which video game were you playing rather than counting birds?"

Raked Over the Coals

Farel was enjoying the music coming through his earphones so much that he forgot to take off his gloves when he went inside.

It was November, and the last of the leaves had just come down. This was the perfect day to rake them, Farel's father had said—sunny and not too hot or too cold, and not windy. Besides, the leaf-collector truck was coming on Monday, in two days.

Farel's father also had suggested that he wear work gloves for the job to prevent blisters, and Farel didn't notice he was still wearing the gloves until he had reached into the dishwasher for a clean glass. He filled the glass from the sink, took a sip and headed back outside. He put the glass on the railing of the deck and went back to raking leaves.

It was getting to be a long job, especially since his dog, Jessica, and little brother, Wally, kept playing in the leaf piles. After raking in the front of the house for a while, Farel came back for a drink of his water. But the glass was empty.

"Did you drink my water?" Farel asked.

"No!" Wally said.

"Then who did?"

"Must have been Jessica," Wally said.

"Don't blame the dog," Farel said. "I know you drank the water."

"Oh, yeah? Then prove it!" Wally said.

Farel held the glass up to the sunlight. "It had to be you," he said to Wally. "I got this glass out of the dishwasher, so no one touched it except me and whoever else drank from it. I've been wearing gloves so I didn't leave these fingerprints on it. And it was on the railing where Jessica couldn't reach it. Besides, dogs don't have fingerprints. So how about getting me another glass of water?"

Picture This

At the end of their two weeks at camp, five girls promised to stay in touch, even though they lived in different parts of the country. They all had email at home and decided that was the best way. They had become close friends because they all liked to play tricks on each other.

In early August, Alexis got the first email, from Ali. It read, "Hi Alexis. After camp, my family went on a vacation and we went through Death Valley, one of the hottest and driest places in the world. This day, we couldn't go anywhere, though, because it was so foggy." The attached picture showed a desert in the fog.

The next email came from Cooper. "Dear Alexis," it said, "you'll never believe this, but last week we had a rainstorm and hail came down! Can you believe it! Hail in the summer in Virginia!" There was a picture of a back porch covered with ice.

Then one came from Zulema. "Here's a picture of me in our garden," it said. It showed Zulema picking blueberries off a vine.

Finally, there was one from Giselle. "My brother and I went fishing at a lake last week and guess what—he caught a lobster. It was delicious," Giselle wrote to Alexis. The picture showed Giselle and a boy with a fishing pole and a lobster dangling from the end of the line.

Alexis sent out an email to all of them. It said, "I see that three of you are still big jokers, and that only one of you sent me a real picture."

Her email continued, "Ali, Zulema and Giselle, you guys are really good at using that software that lets you change pictures. In the desert, it's too hot and dry for fog, especially in the summer. Even if a little formed somehow, it would not stay all day. Plus, blueberries grow on bushes, not on vines. And lobsters are found in salt water, not fresh water. But in a thunderstorm, hail sometimes does come down, even in the South. I hope it didn't break anything, Cooper."

Weight Debate

"Wow, these books weigh a ton," April said as she put another stack on her bed.

She was packing for a plane trip to visit her cousins. One of them was a few years younger than April and was reading a book series that April had read. April had loved those books too, and had a large collection of them. But now she had outgrown them, and she was glad to give them to her cousin.

April's friend, Lea, was helping her pack. April's parents had given her the choice of two suitcases from the same set, one large and one small. In addition to the books, she had laid out everything else she needed for the week.

"What did you say the weight limit is for the airplane?" Lea asked.

"Just 50 pounds or 23kg." Above that they charge you more," April said.

They packed everything into the small suitcase and weighed it on the bathroom scale. It was just a hair under the limit.

"It's light enough but it's a really tight squeeze," April said. "I think I'll use the bigger one."

It was time for Lea to go. As she left, April was moving everything into the large suitcase.

After April returned from the trip, she called Lea. "You'll never believe this, but my suitcase weighed too much and we had to pay extra!" April said. "My parents are taking it out of my allowance! That is so not fair! Somebody's scale is wrong."

"That wasn't the problem," Lea said.

"Then what happened?" April asked.

"Did you weigh the bigger suitcase after you filled it?" Lea asked.

"Why should I? I just put in the same stuff from the smaller one," April said.

"The contents weighed the same, but the bigger suitcase is heavier than the smaller one," Lea said. "When you're weighing something that's in a container, you have to make sure you know the weight of the container."

Alarming Situation

"Where did you get that alarm clock, an antique store?" David laughed.

Andy was a little embarrassed. It was his first time camping, and he hadn't really known what to bring.

The other boys gathered around to look. It was nearly five p.m. and they were taking a break, sitting on the bunk beds in the cabin where they all would sleep the next two nights.

In a few minutes, it would be time to go cook their suppers over the campfire. Later on, they would pack their backpacks. Tomorrow morning, they were going on a hike up the mountain to a lake where they could go swimming.

It would be a long hike, so they would need to get up early. That was why Andy had pulled out the wind-up alarm clock he brought.

"Actually, that thing's a good idea," Jamal said. "With a wind-up clock, you don't have to worry about batteries going dead on you out here in the woods where you can't buy new ones."

Andy appreciated the support. "Let's see, we want to be on our way by eight, so I guess seven o'clock should do it," he said, turning the alarm arrow to seven and pulling the knob to set it.

As the others filed out, Jamal took Andy aside and whispered to him, "That alarm clock is not going to wake us up at seven o'clock tomorrow morning."

"Why not?" Andy asked.

"Wind-up clocks don't know the difference between a.m. and p.m.," Jamal said. "It's going to go off at seven o'clock tonight. If you don't want to put up with David laughing at you again, wait until after seven o'clock to set it."

BONUS SECTION

Five More Minutes
of Science Mysteries!

Water on the Brain

Wade, Leonard, Charles and Robert had come back to the cabin to change before dinner. They were at summer camp, and the afternoon activity period had just ended. The four friends each had decided on a different activity. The activities at that time were rock climbing, swimming, water-balloon tag and horseback riding. They had written the four choices on four slips of paper. They each picked one and didn't tell the others where they were going.

Wade had gotten the paper that said horseback riding. When he returned to the cabin, the others already were there, all of them with wet hair.

"Let's get going," Leonard said as they heard the bell that was the call to dinner.

"I want to change my shirt first," Wade said. "I'm full of dust from the trail. Actually, I'd like to take a shower but I don't have time."

"Okay, so we know you went horseback riding," Robert said. "Now, tell us where we were, wise guy."

"No problem, just show me your hands," Wade said.

They did so.

"Charles, I see your fingers look pretty raw," Wade said. "Leonard, I see that your fingertips are wrinkled. That tells me everything I need to know."

"So, tell us what you know," Charles said.

"Charles, those marks on your fingers mean you were rock-climbing—you wouldn't scratch up your fingers swimming or playing balloon tag. You must have gotten dirty and taken a shower when you got back," Wade said. "You only get wrinkles on your fingers from being in the water a long time. Getting hit with water balloons doesn't cause that, and neither does taking a shower. So Leonard with the wrinkled fingers was the one swimming, which means that Robert was playing water-balloon tag."

2 Pointing Out the Facts

The construction at Powhatan School had just gotten under way. A new wing of classrooms was being added, and a new playground. But the old playground was gone already. Where it once stood was a big hole in the ground.

The pile of dirt that had been dug out was supposed to be off-limits. But the students couldn't resist climbing on it during break time.

Scrambling to the top, Adam felt his foot hit something hard. When he looked down, he thought it was just a rock. He picked it up and looked closer. It seemed to be man-made, reddish brown in color, about the size of a finger and pointed at the end. He rubbed it but it was so encrusted with dirt that he couldn't tell what it was.

"I think it's an arrowhead. Does anybody know what was here before this was a school?" he asked when a couple of friends came up to him.

"This was woods, but way back there was a Native American village near here," Mary Claire said. "That's how the school got its name, for the Powhatans."

Dominic came up to look. "Yeah, but they made their arrowheads out of stone. This looks like metal. Maybe iron. That would mean it's not that old. Probably some modern bow-and-arrow hunter dropped it when this was a forest."

"It's kind of the color of a lot of these rocks," Adam said. "I can't tell what it is, stone or metal."

"I can," Mary Claire said.

"How?" Adam asked.

After break time, she asked the science teacher if she could borrow a magnet. The arrowhead was attracted to it. "If it were made of stone, it wouldn't be magnetic, and then it might be a real arrowhead," Mary Claire said. "Sorry, Adam, this isn't an authentic old arrowhead."

Thrown a Curve

"No kidding, your coach taught you how to throw a curve ball?" Wayne asked.

"Yep," Randy said.

Randy was a good athlete. He was quarterback for his football team in the fall, point guard for his basketball team in the winter and pitcher for his baseball team in the spring.

"I thought you weren't allowed to throw curve balls until you got older," said Wayne.

"The rule actually is that you can only throw so many curve balls in a practice or a game," Randy said. "Because throwing too many can hurt your arm."

"Can you show me how?" Wayne asked.

They were standing in the school courtyard at break time after lunch. The problem was they didn't have a baseball, just a smooth ball about the size and weight of a baseball.

"Okay, you grip it like this," Randy said, showing Wayne how to position his fingers. "When you throw it, you snap your hand down to put topspin on it. Like this." Randy threw the ball with a downward snap of his wrist, but the ball just went straight.

Wayne retrieved the ball after it bounced off the brick wall and handed it back to Randy. "Try again," Wayne said.

Randy did, snapping his wrist harder this time. But still the ball went straight.

After three more tries with the same result, Randy said, "The ball was really curving for me at practice last night. What's happening?"

"At practice, you were using a real baseball, which has stitches that are above the surface of the ball," Wayne said. "The stitches are what grab into the air when you put topspin on the ball by snapping your wrist. Because of the topspin, air is moved out of the way under the ball, lowering the air pressure there, and more air is brought around to the top of the ball, raising the air pressure there. The result is the ball curves down. It's the same reason golf balls have dimples—to grab the air. Except in golf, backspin is put on the ball and the dimples help it go up. This ball is smooth, so you don't get that effect."

The Long Run

"One lap to decide the fastest runner in the school! In the world! In the universe!"

Scooter liked to talk that way, but in fact the race had become a big deal between the classes. They enjoyed challenging each other to contests—who could make more free throws in a minute, who could punt a football the farthest, who could do more chin-ups.

After school, a group from both classes had gathered at the track. Each class had picked its fastest runner—Nathan and Jay. Nathan was probably faster in a short distance but Jay had better endurance, so everyone thought that one lap would be a fair contest.

They flipped a coin, and Nathan got the inner lane.

"Both of you stay in your lane. No cutting each other off," said Scooter, whom everyone trusted as a fair official.

He lined them up next to each other. "On your marks, get set, go!"

Nathan and Jay took off, running at top speed at first, but then slowing down a bit after the first burst of energy wore off. Nathan was ahead as they went down the straight part on the other side of the field, but by the time they rounded the second turn, Jay had caught up. They crossed the finish line together as everyone cheered.

"A tie!" Scooter said. "Okay, rest a few minutes and then you can race again to see who's faster."

"We don't have to," Nathan said. "Isn't it obvious who's faster?"

"Jay was in the lane outside of me," Nathan said. "The outside lane is the same distance in the straight parts, but it's a longer distance around the curves. Since we both started at the same place and stayed in our lanes all the way around the track, Jay went farther than I did. Since he went farther in the same amount of time, he ran faster."

Occupational Hazards

It was the start of Career Week in science class. The students had to pick an area of science they found interesting and then research what it would be like to work in that job.

"J.L., let's start with you," said their teacher, Mr. Chisek. "What career are you going to study?"

"I've always liked space," J.L. said. "I think meteors are really neat. So I'm going to look into being a meteorologist."

"I like space, too," George said. "I just love looking at the stars. So I'll research being an astrologer."

Mr. Chisek said, "How about something a little more down to Earth?"

"I'm interested in plants," Jahari said. "I'm going to do my report on how to be a botanist."

"Is there anyone interested in rocks and minerals?" the teacher asked.

"Me," Trisha said. "I'll do mine on what it's like to be a geographer."

"Anyone interested in electronics?" Mr. Chisek asked.

Brandon raised his hand. "I love messing around with radios. I'm going to research radiology," he said.

Tucker leaned over and whispered to Acquan, "I'm surprised Mr. Chisek isn't saying anything. But I guess he's going to let them find out the hard way. All of them except for one are in for a surprise."

"I know what you mean," Acquan said. "Meteorology is not the study of meteors, it's the study of weather. And astrology isn't the study of the universe, astronomy is. Astrology isn't a science, it's a belief that the stars and planets affect our personalities and our lives."

Tucker said, "Trisha will soon find out that geology is the study of things found in the ground and that geography is the study of the Earth's physical features. And radiology isn't about radios, it's about using X-rays and radioactive substances to detect and treat disease. Jahari is the only one who's right; botany is about studying plants. Being accurate is really important in science!"

Discover
One Minute Mysteries:
65 Short Mysteries You Solve With Math!

1

Cereal Numbers

Ron and Lauren's father had made a New Year's resolution in 2008 to be healthier. Part of his program, along with exercising, was eating only cereal for breakfast instead of things like bacon and eggs.

It had taken him a while to find a kind of cereal he liked, but finally on the first day of February he settled on one. It happened to be Ron and Lauren's favorite too.

He even had his own special box of it, which he labeled with a marker: "Dad's Box—Not for Kids." The box held 700 grams of cereal, and by measuring out a cup a day, he'd made the cereal last exactly one month. So he decided that he'd start a new box on the first of each month.

One day in late March the family sat down to breakfast together. Their father looked into his box and frowned.

"I don't think I'll have enough to make it through the month," he said.

He looked at Ron and Lauren. "This reminds me of Goldilocks and the Three Bears," he said. "Someone's been eating my cereal," he said in a deep voice.

"No we haven't, Dad," Ron and Lauren said together.

"Then what happened to my cereal?" he asked.

"The first box lasted all of February, which has 28 days this year—every four years it has 29," Lauren said.

"But March has 31 days," Ron added. "So to make this month's 700-gram box last 31 days, you should have been taking out a little less each day."

Lauren did some quick division on a sheet of paper. "To make 700 grams last 28 days, the measuring cup must hold 25 grams of this cereal," Lauren said.

Ron also did some division. "You should have been taking 22.58 grams, to be exact. But don't worry, we'll give you some from our box."

2

Jumping Through Hoops

Ms. O'Cork, the girls' P.E. teacher, tried to mix up the activities to give her class different kinds of exercise.

Today, she had brought out a bunch of hula hoops for warm-ups, which the girls enjoyed.

They were out on the back field. Because it was used for all kinds of sports, the field had no distance markings.

After warm-ups, Ms. O'Cork gathered everyone on the edge of the field, where she dropped a large bag of soccer balls and some short tape measures, the kind used to measure people for clothes.

"The school record for punting a soccer ball is 45 yards," she announced. "Anyone who can break the record in the next two minutes and can prove it doesn't have to run laps later."

"But it will take that long just to measure 45 yards with these little tape measures," someone said.

"Okay, anyone who can figure out how to accurately measure the distance in that time doesn't have to run laps either," the teacher said.

Jasmine turned to Audrey, who was the goalie on their soccer team and a good punter. "I know a way we'll both get out of running laps," Jasmine said.

"What do you have in mind?" asked Audrey.

Jasmine used the tape measure to measure the circumference of a hula hoop, starting at the joint where the two ends joined. It was 108 inches around.

"Dividing 108 inches by 12 inches (the equivalent of 1 foot) means the hula hoop is 9 feet around, or 3 yards," Jasmine said. "I'll roll it along the ground. Every time the joint comes that's three yards farther. Forty-five yards divided by 3 yards per roll is 15. So after fifteen rolls of the hula hoop, I'll be 45 yards away. Warm up that kicking leg!"

Flooring Them

3

Lily and Robert agreed with their parents that it was time to replace the worn-out kitchen floor. It was cracked, stained and impossible to clean.

But picking new tile was a different matter. Their parents had brought home a half-dozen samples from the tile store and laid them out around the kitchen. Although the floor was 10 feet by 12 feet and the samples were each only 1 square foot, they were big enough to get a feel for how they would look.

In the end it came down to a choice of two kinds of tiles. The imitation granite tiles came in boxes of 25 for $100 a box. The imitation marble tiles came in boxes of 50 for $150 a box. In both cases, they had to buy an entire box, and unused tiles couldn't be returned for a refund.

Everyone in the family agreed they liked the two kinds equally—the decision was just a matter of which was cheaper.

"Let's buy the granite ones," Robert said. "We'll have a lot less left over."

"But aren't we trying to save money?" Lily asked.

"That's what I meant," Robert said.

"Well, that's what I meant, too, and I think we should go with the marble ones," she said.

As usual, the argument ended with an appeal to their parents.

"Okay, each of you tell us why you think one tile will save more money than the other," their father said.

Robert said, "Well, the area that needs to be covered is 10 feet by 12 feet. That's 120 square feet, or ten times twelve. If we buy the granite tiles, which come in boxes of 25, we'd need five boxes; five times 25 is 125. We'd have five tiles left over, 125 minus 120. Since it costs $100 for a box of 25, each tile costs $4, or 100 divided by 25. With five left over, we're wasting $20, five leftover tiles times $4 apiece.

He continued, "With the marble tiles, there's 50 in a box, so we'd need three boxes to cover the 120 square feet, three times 50 is 150. We'd have 30 left over, or 150 tiles minus 120 square feet. Since those boxes cost $150 each, each tile costs $3, or $150 divided by 50. So we'd be wasting $90, thirty leftover tiles times $3 apiece."

"True," Lily said, "but it's a question of how much we're spending in total. The five boxes of granite tiles would cost $500, or five times $100. The three boxes of marble tiles would cost only $450, three times $150. So we'd be saving $50 by buying the marble tiles, even though we would have more tiles left over."

"Lily's idea actually would save us money," their mother said. "Let's go with the marble tiles."

4

Toss-Up

"These cookies must be for me," Dylan said.

"No, they must be for me," Isaac said.

Dylan and Isaac's travel basketball team had stopped for dinner at Dylan's house after a game. Dylan's mother had made a fantastic dinner, and everyone except Dylan and Isaac was too full for the cookies Dylan's father had baked.

Isaac said, "Let's toss for them. Cookie by cookie." He got out a quarter. "I'll toss, you call," he said.

"Heads," Dylan said.

It came up tails. Isaac ate a cookie.

"Heads," Dylan called on the second toss.

Tails again. Isaac ate another cookie.

"Heads," Dylan called again.

It came up tails again. Isaac ate a third cookie.

By now the other boys were snickering. "Heads again," Dylan said.

Tails once more.

"Maybe you should start calling tails," Isaac suggested. "I'm getting pretty full, eating all these cookies."

"No, I'll stick with heads," Dylan said. "I mean, what are the odds that it will come up tails again?"

"I can tell you the odds exactly," Isaac said.

Dylan looked surprised. "How did you figure it out that fast?" he asked.

"The chances are even that on any coin toss, either heads or tails will come up," Isaac said. "It doesn't matter what happened on any previous tosses. The odds are still 50-50 that it will come up one way or the other the next time.

"By the way," Isaac added, "it's easy to figure out the odds of a coin always coming up one way or the other on a number of coin tosses in a row. You double the result each time. The chance of a coin coming up one way or the other is one in two on the first toss. The chance of it coming up the same way each time is one in four for two tosses, one in eight for three tosses, one in 16 for four tosses, one in 32 for five tosses, and so on. But that's just the odds against that happening in general. On any given toss of the coin, the odds are always 50-50."

5

Paper Chase

"What do they use this thing for, anyway—to weigh trucks?" Diego asked his lab partner Jenna.

The science lab had several good scales, including a triple-beam scale that measured with accuracy down to 0.1 grams.

But their teacher, Mr. Holmes, had gotten out the old scales for this assignment. He said he was going to order new shelves for the storage room and needed to know how strong they had to be to hold the packages of paper he kept there. Each package was 500 pages. He wanted to know exactly how much a sheet weighed.

The students thought that would be easy enough to figure out, until Mr. Holmes made them use the old scales. They could hold a lot of weight but were accurate only to ten grams.

Jenna laid a sheet of paper on the scale. It didn't budge. She tried another. This time the balance moved.

"So two sheets is about ten grams, meaning one sheet is five grams. More or less," Diego said.

"He's not looking for a 'more or less' answer," Jenna said.

"Well, then, there's only one thing we can do," he said.

"What's that?" asked Jenna.

"Let's get some more paper," Diego said. They went into the storage room and returned with two full packages of 500 sheets each, unwrapped the packages and put the paper on the scale, after removing the original two sheets. The weight came to 5,440 grams.

"Since 1,000 sheets weigh 5,440 grams, the weight of each sheet is one-thousandth of that. To divide by 1,000, all we have to do is move the decimal point three places to the left. So one sheet is 5.44 grams," Diego said.

"I see, just because the scale is imprecise doesn't mean we have to be," Jenna said.

Index

Photo and Illustration Credits

About the Authors

Eric Yoder is a writer and editor who has been published in a variety of magazines, newspapers, newsletters and online publications on science, government, law, business, sports and other topics. He has written, contributed to or edited numerous books, mainly in the areas of employee benefits and financial planning. A reporter at *The Washington Post* who also does freelance writing and editing, he was a member of the Advisory Committee for Science, Naturally's *101 Things Everyone Should Know About Science*. He and his wife, Patti, have two daughters, Natalie and Valerie. He can be reached at Eric@ScienceNaturally.com.

Natalie Yoder is a high-school student whose favorite subjects are math, science and English. A sports enthusiast, she participates in gymnastics, field hockey, soccer and diving. She also enjoys reading, writing, playing the clarinet, playing with the family beagle, Trevor, and listening to music. She loved helping to create and shape these science mysteries. She is hoping to work in advertising after college. She can be reached at Natalie@ScienceNaturally.com.

About Science, Naturally!®

Science, Naturally! is committed to increasing science literacy by exploring and demystifying key science topics. Our mission is to produce products—for children and adults alike—that are filled with interesting facts, important insights and key connections in science. Our materials are designed to make potentially intimidating topics intriguing and accessible. Our products are perfect for kids, parents, educators and anyone interested in gaining a better understanding of how science affects everyday life.

Our first title, *If My Mom Were a Platypus: Mammal Babies and their Mothers,* won an "NSTA Recommends" award from the National Science Teachers' Association and has been featured by the American Association for the Advancement of Science and the Carnegie Academy for Science Education as well as in science, children's and natural history museums around the country.

101 Things Everyone Should Know About Science was our second release. Key concepts in biology, chemistry, physics, earth science and general science are explored and demystified. Endorsed by science organizations and educators, this easy-to-tackle book is a powerful tool to assess and increase science literacy. Finishing touches are now being put on *101 Things Everyone Should Know About Math*, a great tool that makes understanding math easy and fun. It is also our first math title.

We are very excited to introduce you to our latest book: *One Minute Mysteries: 65 Short Mysteries You Solve With Science!* This book is the perfect addition to our line of products that make learning science fun! Watch for the next title in the series: *One Minute Mysteries: 65 Short Mysteries You Solve With Math!* Odds are, you'll love this one!

For more information about our publications, to request a catalog or to be added to our mailing list, visit us at ScienceNaturally.com or give us a call.

Teaching the science of everyday life

Science, Naturally!®
627 A Street, NE
Washington, DC 20002
202-465-4798
Toll-free: 1-866-SCI-9876
(1-866-724-9876)
Fax: 202-558-2132
Info@ScienceNaturally.com
www.ScienceNaturally.com

If you enjoyed this book, check out our other publications:

One Minute Mysteries:
65 Short Mysteries You Solve With Math!
By Eric Yoder and Natalie Yoder

The second book in our wildly successful "One Minute Mysteries" series, *One Minute Mysteries: 65 Short Mysteries You Solve With Math!* keeps you entertained and eager to learn more! These short mysteries, each just one minute long, have a fun and interesting twist—you have to tap into your mathematical wisdom to solve them! Solve 65 math brain twisters (solutions included) that challenge your knowledge of math in everyday life! Bonus section includes five more mysteries from our next title in the series.

As much fun as the first book in the series, *One Minute Mysteries: 65 Short Mysteries You Solve With Science!,* this educational book is easy to use at home, in school or even in the car. Great for kids, grown-ups, educators and anyone who loves good mysteries, good math problems or both!

Fun mysteries for kids and adults!

Boost your child's math knowledge!

Over 60 mysteries with solutions included!

One Minute Mysteries: 65 Short Mysteries You Solve With Math!
By Eric Yoder and Natalie Yoder
Recommended for ages 10-14
ISBN: 0-9678020-0-8
Paperback $9.95

101 Things Everyone Should Know About Science
By Dia L. Michels and Nathan Levy

Why do you see lightning before you hear thunder? What keeps the planets orbiting around the Sun? Why do we put salt on roads when they are icy? What metal is a liquid at room temperature? And the burning question: Why do so many scientists wear white lab coats?

Science affects everything—yet so many of us wish we understood it better. Using an accessible question-and-answer approach, *101 Things Everyone Should Know About Science* expands a reader's knowledge–whether you're 8 or 108. Key concepts in biology, chemistry, physics, earth science and general science are explored and demystified by an award-winning science writer and a seasoned educational trainer in consultation with a team of scientists. Endorsed by science organizations and educators, this easy-to-tackle book is a powerful tool to assess and increase science literacy. Perfect for kids, parents, grown-ups and anyone interested in gaining a better understanding of how science impacts everyday life.

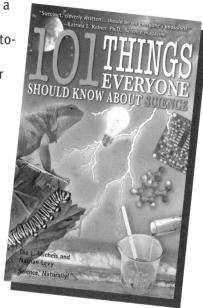

101 Things Everyone Should Know About Science
By Dia L. Michels and
Nathan Levy
Recommended for ages 8-12
ISBN 0-9678020-5-9
Paperback $9.95

101 Things Everyone Should Know About Math
By Marc Zev, Kevin Segal, and Nathan Levy

Using a simple question-and-answer format and focusing on real-life situations, *101 Things Everyone Should Know About Math* is an easy and fun-to-use tool designed to broaden your understanding of math. Whether you're 8 or 108, this book will help you as you use math each day. The second in the "101 Things Everyone Should Know" series, this book helps readers of all ages enjoy and understand basic mathematical operations. Mathematical concepts are explained, simplified and applied to real-life situations, so even the most "math-averse" person will feel more confident as they use math. Written by author/educators Marc Zev, Kevin Segal and Nathan Levy, *101 Things Everyone Should Know About Math* is perfect for kids, parents, grown-ups, students, teachers and anyone interested in the difference between an Olympic score of 9.0 and an earthquake registering 9.0.

Explore a variety of math concepts using fun, everyday topics like:

Food and nutrition
Travel
Sports and Recreation

Music and Art
Nature
Health

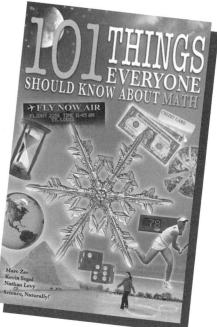

Marc Zev is an engineer and founder of the Foundation for Innovative Learning.

Kevin Segal is an actuary with a Master's in Applied Mathematics.

Nathan Levy is a seasoned educator and author of numerous books on education.

101 Things Everyone Should Know About Math
By Marc Zev, Kevin Segal and Nathan Levy
Recommended for ages 10-14
ISBN: 0-9678020-3-2
Paperback $9.95

If My Mom Were a Platypus:
Mammal Babies and Their Mothers
By Dia L. Michels • Illustrated by Andrew Barthelmes

"As engaging visually as it is verbally!"
—Dr. Ines Cifuentes, Carnegie Academy for Science Education

"The animal facts . . . are completely engrossing. Most readers are sure to be surprised by something they learn about these seemingly familiar animals."
—Carolyn Baile, *ForeWord* magazine

NSTA recommends™
NATIONAL SCIENCE TEACHERS ASSOCIATION

Middle grade students learn how 14 mammals are born, eat, sleep, learn and mature. The fascinating facts depict how mammal infants begin life dependent on their mothers and grow to be self-sufficient adults. This book highlights the topics of birth, growth, knowledge and eating for 13 different animals. All stories are told from the baby's point of view. The 14th and final species is a human infant, with amazing similarities to the other stories. With stunning full color and black-and-white illustrations and concise information, this book helps children develop a keen sense of what makes mammals special.

Recommended for ages 8-12.Curiculum-based activity guide with dozens of fun, hands-on projects available free of charge at www.ScienceNaturally.com

ISBN: 1-930775-35-0	Hardback book	$16.95
ISBN: 1-930775-44-X	Hardback + 15" plush platypus	$29.95
ISBN: 1-930775-19-9	Paperback book	$ 9.95
ISBN: 1-930775-30-X	Paperback + 15" plush platypus	$22.95